Call Me Bill!

A TRUE STORY

C. Nolan Phillips

WestBow
P R E S S
A DIVISION OF THOMAS NELSON

WestBow Press books may be ordered through booksellers or by contacting:

WestBow Press
A Division of Thomas Nelson
1663 Liberty Drive
Bloomington, IN 47403
www.westbowpress.com
1-(866) 928-1240

ISBN: 978-1-4497-6577-4 (sc)
ISBN: 978-1-4497-6578-1 (e)

Library of Congress Control Number: 2012918207

Printed in the United States of America

WestBow Press rev. date: 11/16/2012

Contents

Prologue...ix

Chapter 1. Your Baby Is Dead.................................1

Chapter 2. A Functional Alcoholic 15

Chapter 3. A Family Crisis 19

Chapter 4. Born for Trouble 29

Chapter 5. Call Me Bill!......................................39

Chapter 6. State School.......................................45

Chapter 7. House of Horror...................................55

Chapter 8. Sandy's Story: The School.......................59

Chapter 9. A Typical Day.....................................65

Chapter 10. Christmas 71

Chapter 11. A Ray of Hope....................................77

Chapter 12. Billy's Story 79

Chapter 13. State School Friends............................87

Chapter 14. Next Step...91

Chapter 15. Release from Half-Way......................................95

Chapter 16. Return to Columbus...103

Chapter 17. Hitting Bottom...109

Chapter 18. Free at Last 111

Chapter 19. Betty's Story...119

Chapter 20. Don's Story 127

Chapter 21. Rescuing the Perishing....................................129

Chapter 22. Fresh Start..133

Chapter 23. Baby Steps..137

Chapter 24. Before and After 143

Chapter 25. He's Still Working on Me 149

Chapter 26. Friends on the Outside 155

Chapter 27. Bill and Sheena 163

Chapter 28. Spreading the Good News................................171

Chapter 29. Another Miracle 183

Chapter 30. The Family 189

Chapter 31. Have Things Changed?....................................193

Chapter 32. Tribute from Bill's Son 197

Chapter 33. Bill's Worldview..199

Chapter 34. Postlude..207

IN APPRECIATION OF---
Harold Smith
Beloved friend and pastor
Who brought me the Good News
That I was deeply loved by God.
—Billy Reid

Prologue

PRIOR to 1960 thousands of children with emotional and physical handicaps received little treatment throughout America. Some, abandoned by their families made their way into treatment centers for the handicapped simply because they were unmanageable. The Columbus Developmental Center, also known as Columbus State School, was one such treatment center. Located near the heart of the capitol city of the eleventh largest state in the nation, Columbus State School received children as young as six years of age. Housed with other physically and mentally challenged individuals in open dormitories, the residents ranged from six to fifty years in age. An unknown number of these were at least of average intelligence and physical ability. As many as forty residents were assigned to a room. The deplorable conditions were enough to drive an ordinary person to despair and insanity. Social rehabilitation and development were limited. With limited supervision, physical and sexual abuse was common.

Routinely told by caregivers he would never leave the institution he was confined to, one thirteen-year-old boy determined to find a way out of this madness. Billy Reid was one of the lost children sent away by family and locked up by community and state until he convinced authorities he was able to care for himself. This is his story witnessed by some who knew him.

The Bible says that God is "...the God who performs wonders." Bill Reid's life is proof of that. Told by his family that he was born for trouble, Billy Reid believed it. To be exact, the trouble started three days before he was born and continued for twenty-six tormented years until an incredible change-----a miracle---happened. In an amazing series of events that continue to the writing of this story, God performed incredible miracles in Bill Reid's life.

Bill Reid is an example of the transforming power of Jesus Christ. While many live through painful life experiences failing to realize a fraction of their potential, Bill inspires hope in those who have lost their child-like ability to believe in miracles. Miracles still happen for him and many whom the world has written off as damaged goods. They are living proof that despair can be transformed into full and meaningful life.

Finally released from confinement Billy found himself still locked within a prison without bars, one made of bitterness. His hatred for those who had abandoned him and those who had abused him threatened to destroy him. Twice driven to the brink of suicide, he was miraculously freed from his destructive intent to find a meaningful life. The greatest miracle was not his release from State School but the removal of the bars of bitterness that held him.

You may know someone like this. It could be you. Billy's story is an attempt to explore the hidden, secret world where unknown numbers of people born with physical and emotional handicaps, are locked away and forgotten by the outside world. It is a glimpse into the destructive prison of hatred and how one man escaped the chains of both prisons.

Crushing circumstances are often the cause and excuse for meaningless life. Billy Reid refused to let his circumstances keep him from living a purposeful life. Unable to find purpose and meaning through his own effort, a personal encounter with God changed his life and gave him the boldness with which he now shares his life with others.

By that miracle Billy discovered a worldview that many overlook. God delights in finding those who believe in Him and demonstrates His power in them. "For the eyes of the LORD run to and fro throughout the whole earth, to show Himself strong on behalf of *those* whose heart *is* loyal to Him." Some overcome their circumstances by human effort, intervention of others, or a combination of events. Bill escaped his prison of hate and bitterness through the sheer grace of God and the discovery that God loved him.

Some people change gradually over years. Billy Reid changed miraculously in a single moment that can only be explained by the intervention of God. It was not until Billy had exhausted all his energy and schemes and given up on living that God revealed His love to him and saved him from certain death at his own hands. As Billy often said, "God did it! I couldn't"!

Your Baby Is Dead.

"MRS. Reid, I'm afraid your baby is dead." The doctor's words confirmed the dread growing in Esther Reid's mind ever since the accident in her kitchen two days earlier. Her unborn child had been injured. Its miraculous survival three days later would be a bitter sweet relief. Weighing barely two pounds and two ounces, suffering from pre-natal injuries caused by the kitchen accident, the baby boy would test the Reid family's emotional resources over the next twenty-six years.

Earl Reid moved his family into Ravenna, an Ohio crossroads community, located in the Snowbelt of Northeast, Ohio. Earl and Esther would eventually raise ten children. Located approximately eighteen miles East of Akron and thirty-five miles Southeast of Cleveland, Ravenna borrowed its name from a small town in Italy. It was founded in 1799 and developed over the next two hundred years. Ravenna was and still is a blend of century-old architecture, modern buildings and industry. A bustling Northeastern Ohio town, it is a small slice of Americana where people congregate, converse, and do business. It was here that Billy Reid was born.

In 1877, Henry Parsons Crowell, owner of the Quaker Mill in Ravenna, became the first to market and register a trademark for cereal; the Quaker symbol. By 1943, the start of Billy's life, Quaker sales reached $90 million. Wartime demand for the company's famous oats pumped new life into the company and employment for many local residents.

Prior to the move to Ravenna, the Reid family lived in Geneva, another small town with small town charm. Billy was born in Charden, a small community, seven miles outside Ravenna. It lacked a store or gas station to supply its needs. The family home lacked electricity or a telephone but there was plenty of room for the growing family with a large back lot and chicken house. A painter by trade, Earl moved his wife, Esther, and their eight children from Geneva to Charden where he found employment in an arsenal factory at Ravenna working seven days a week.

During World War II, Ravenna was the site of the Ravenna Arsenal. Workers at the Ravenna Arsenal produced more weapons for the war effort than any other plant in the United States. More than 14,000 Ohioans found employment there during World War II. The arsenal eventually included 1,371 buildings on 21,418 acres. The complex ceased arms production at the end of World War II and began making fertilizer. With the outbreak of the Korean War, the Ravenna Arsenal resumed production of arms under the direction of the Firestone Company. In 1957, the Arsenal stopped munitions production. It was reopened during the Vietnam War and again became a munitions production center. Much of the Ravenna Arsenal in the late '90s was the Ohio National Guard's Ravenna Training and Logistics Site.

In 1940 the war in Europe and the Pacific was full scale and war-time production was booming in the local munitions factory. When the Reid family moved there, they never wanted for necessities with Earl's employment. The two-story frame house compensated for the lack of indoor plumbing, electricity or telephone service with its spacious rooms. The family passed an uneventful winter there in 1943. The house provided comfortable shelter from the sub-zero winds that swept across the interior countryside from Lake Eire.

Esther Reid was born in Charden, Ohio, May 22, 1908. She was born at home. She met Earl Reid who was born September 27, 1907 in Cleveland, Ohio. They married on June 30, 1927. They met in Geneva. Earl was scotch. His grandmother was Irish. His grandfather was Scotch. Earl's grandmother was born in Germany. Esther's father came from Norway. Her mother's family fought in the revolutionary war against England. Her grandfather served General Leavenworth. The Reid family was a mixture of European immigrants of German, Irish, Scottish, and English blood.

Esther was in her sixth month of pregnancy. It was Sunday morning, March 21, 1943. Winters in Ohio were bitter cold. The drab appearance of the flat fields was just starting to show a hint of green. Easter would be late this year, not for five more weeks on April 25. She recalled that morning vividly years afterward. "The kids always got excited about Easter and hiding eggs and such. I was in the kitchen getting breakfast for everyone that morning. I didn't see the kid's marbles on the kitchen floor. I guess they had left them there the night before. The first thing I remember was my feet flying out from under me. I didn't have time to reach for a chair or table before I fell against the corner of the kitchen table and onto the floor. The table was solid and didn't give a bit as my side hit it. It really jolted me. I felt a sharp pain when I hit the porcelain covered table. I remember shouting, 'Earl, I'm hurt'."

"Earl ran into the kitchen to help me up. I could barely get my breath, the pain was so bad. I thought at first that I had broken some ribs. I pressed my hand to my side tenderly to see if any ribs were broken. "

"Earl knew I was hurt. His voice was shaking when he said, 'Let me help you into a chair.' He maneuvered me toward a table chair but the pain was so bad I let out an awful moan. Earl tried to make me feel better. He said, 'I'm going to get you into bed, Esther. You may have hurt the baby, too.' I couldn't hide the pain from him. I said, 'I don't think so. I'll be alright in a while. Just help me upstairs and let me rest'."

"With Earl helping I managed to get up the stairs to our bedroom and eased into the bed as best I could. I stayed in bed all that day. Betty Sue, my oldest child, organized the kids and kept them quiet the rest of the day. She was fifteen-years-old but she had been helping me with the kids since she was little. It was the worst Sunday of my life. As long as I stayed still the pain was bearable. My water broke Monday morning waking me from a deep sleep. I was in trouble."

"We had no telephone at the time. There was no way to call a doctor to the house, so Earl drove seven miles to Ravenna to find a phone and call the doctor. He wanted to find the doctor who had assisted in the delivery of my other babies. Apart from the pain in my side from the fall, I wasn't too worried about having this baby. Earl had been with me for the delivery of my eight kids. I knew he could take care of me. I had plenty of experience having babies. We could have this one, too. The only worry I had was the timing. I was only five months into my pregnancy. I didn't know if the baby would survive that early."

Things had changed with the war effort. Lots of doctors were serving in military hospitals. Small towns only had interns and nurses to meet the needs of small communities like Ravenna. Earl was unable to locate the doctor and went to the local Red Cross office for aid. They advised him to find a doctor who would drive out into the country to treat his wife since no ambulance was available to get her into town to the hospital. The doctor told Earl what to do if the baby should come before he got there. Earl wasn't much satisfied with his advice. He found a new doctor who was still in training. The new doctor agreed to come the next morning. The new doctor had never delivered a baby unassisted but he promised to come. Esther recalled, "As I said, I wasn't very concerned because Earl was a good husband. He had been with me in the birth of my other eight and I knew I could count on him if the baby came."

"The doctor came about mid-morning the next day and examined me. He told me I had a mild infection but he kept trying to feel any movement or hear a heartbeat. After what seemed like several minutes he shocked me. 'Mrs. Reid, I believe your baby is dead. Mr. Reid, you need to get your wife to the hospital.' Earl helped me down the stairs and into the car and drove to the closest hospital, Robinson Memorial Hospital, in Ravenna."

Robinson Memorial Hospital began as an 18-bed facility founded in 1894. In later years it grew to a 150 bed hospital serving the city and surrounding area with quality care. In 1943, the nursing staff was stretched thin. Doctors worked long hours to meet the needs of the growing area. The admitting clerk sent Esther to a maternity ward where the nursing staff began to prep her for delivery.

"'Why am I in this maternity ward', I wondered. I called to the first nurse who came into the room and told her, 'The doctor told me he would have to operate because the baby's dead. If I don't have an operation, he said I could die. Why am I in a maternity ward'? Either she didn't know what to say, or she pretended not to know the answer. She just took my temperature and checked my blood pressure and left without saying anything that I remember."

"A few minutes later another nurse came in the ward and told me I had a fever. They were afraid if there was an infection it might be contagious so they were moving me out of the maternity ward."

"There were already several patients being cared for in the halls. Robinson Memorial was small and every bed was taken. They placed me in a three-bed ward. They pulled a curtain around my bed and posted an isolation warning over my bed. I don't know how long it was until the admitting nurse came in and examined my belly. She didn't hear any heartbeat or find any movement from the baby. She gave me a shot the doctor had ordered for infection and medication for pain. I got drowsy and drifted off to sleep. That was about 10:30 PM. The hospital asked all the visitors to leave. I guess they were getting ready to change shifts for the nurses. It was time for the graveyard shift to start."

"I was jerked awake by a sharp pain. I had felt that pain before. I thought, 'Oh, my Lord, I'm in labor'! I remembered the young doctor telling me, 'You won't have any labor pain or contractions because the baby is dead.' I looked at the clock on the wall and it was 11:30 PM. I rang the bell beside the bed for a nurse. A few minutes passed and the night shift nurse came in. She was an older woman. She had been around patients and had experience with new mothers and their anxieties about pregnancy and delivery. She wasn't in any hurry. I can just see her now plodding into the ward. When she came in, I told her, 'I think I'm in labor'!"

Nurses were scarce at Ravenna Community Hospital--- in fact, they were scarce all over Northern Ohio in 1943. A war was in force in Europe and the Pacific Islands. Women who would have found gainful employment as nurses and aids were needed in local factories producing war materials. Available nurses worked long hours. They were responsible for several patients. Esther Reid was one of three patients in the maternity ward that night. There were other wards and patients to attend. Expectant mothers were always anxious about labor. The night shift nurse's examination at the start of the shift assured her this was another false labor. She would make the trip to the semi-darkened ward just to reassure the patient. "Go back to sleep. You're only dreaming," she said. I really bristled, "I have eight children and I know labor pain when I feel it!" The night nurse just raised her voice and said, 'Don't upset the other patients. Go to sleep.' She turned out the light by the bed and stalked away."

"I didn't know what to do. I didn't know who to call for help. I wished Earl were here. He would have set those nurses straight! The pains got worse. They were coming every few minutes. At midnight I couldn't stand it anymore. I rang for the nurse again. 'I'm in labor! Get the doctor!' That really upset her but she called the doctor. A few minutes later he came into the ward and instructed the nurse to bring pills and a hypodermic. Then he said, 'She's going to sleep.' He used his stethoscope to examine me again and said, "No movement, no muscle reaction, no life." Then he gave me the hypodermic himself. I was already woozy from the first pills and I tried again to tell him, 'I have eight children. I know what's going on, you don't!'" The doctor just kept telling me to be still and I fell asleep. It must have been 1:30 AM by then. The pains stopped. I dozed off but in no time I was jolted awake again by more sharp pains. The contractions were coming fast and they were sharp. I didn't know what to do. I didn't know who to call!"

"Nurse! Nurse!" I must have wakened every patient in the maternity ward with my shouts. I was thirty-eight years old and having a baby in a maternity ward and nobody would help me! No one came. I was no novice when it came to having babies. This was my ninth pregnancy. I knew the ins and outs of child-birthing."

"I had been sent to the hospital to terminate my pregnancy and remove the dead baby. The nursing staff was told to keep me in bed for several days. They had done their best to put me to sleep but it's hard to sleep when your abdomen is splitting. I was definitely in labor."

"Nurse! Nurse!" I really yelled this time. The night shift nurse stuck her head in the door and said, 'You, again!' And left the room. That's when I decided, 'They don't believe me! I'll show them.' I remembered the doctor saying that the baby's head was up and its feet were down. I tried to ignore the pain and mumbled to myself, 'You good for nothing….I'll show you!' I sat up in bed, pushed my knees apart and bent with the contractions that were coming in waves. I remember thinking, 'Maybe the baby is alive'!"

"My yelling woke the woman in the bed next to me. She had heard me yelling and rose up on one elbow to see what was going on. When she looked at me, I gave another groan and gasped at her, 'The baby's coming!' I could feel the baby's head pressing through. Water gushed out. I had the pure, painful sensation of bringing another child into the world. Billy came out. I looked down at the stained sheets and saw this tiny form lying there. I thought, 'Is it alive?' I pulled my foot back to gently push the baby out of the way. When I touched him there was no movement. I pushed harder. My foot must have pressed on the baby's back and that's when I heard the tiniest squeal I'd ever heard. It was more like a squeak! But I heard it!"

"I didn't have to push a button! The other two patients in the ward with me did. You could have heard them shouting anywhere in that maternity wing. 'Nurse! Nurse! Come quick!' And they were mad, too! That maternity ward came alive!'"

"I was just sobbing as I bent over Billy's tiny body lying on the sheets. The light from the corridor was shining across the bed. I saw the head nurse's face coming into the room. Her face changed the second she saw my bed. The patient in the bed next to me was waving crazily for the nurse and shouting, 'She's had her baby! It's born!.' The covers were thrown back enough for the nurse to see Billy laying there and as tiny as he was he moved slightly where he lay. I had been admitted to be delivered of a dead fetus. It was obvious that I had had a live birth."

"The head nurse just threw her hands into the air and ran for the doctor. It was 3:15 AM when Billy was born. He weighed a whopping two pounds and two ounces but had a pair of healthy lungs. Had it not been for the premature fall, he most likely would have had a normal birth. When the head nurse picked him up from the bed she showed me the ugly, black and blue mark on his hip. He most likely got that from the fall against the kitchen table three days ago."

From his appearance Billy seemed too tiny to live. The doctor who examined him judged the pregnancy to be about 24 weeks. In 1943, survival for premature babies that young was rare. Sixty years later there would be reported survivals of premature children weighing less than one pound but in 1943 survival at Billy's weight was highly unusual. The doctor and nurse took him straight to an incubator. He was the tiniest preemie there. A shoe box would have made a cradle for him. His head looked the size of a small orange. When the doctor came running into the room the head nurse was holding the baby in her hands. He took one look at her and said, 'Get your hands off that baby. He could be deformed. His bones are still soft.' A preemie as tiny as he was could have suffered serious damage without special care.

"When that head nurse came back from the nursery, I lit into her. I didn't curse but what I did say was plain enough. The Doctor tried to calm me and I told him a few things, too. 'You didn't know any better, but she knew better.' I was beside myself. The doctor saw it and gave me a shot that put me to sleep."

"The next day the doctor came back into my room and told me that my son was strong but needed special care. He was very apologetic for all that happened. Earl and I held no ill feeling toward the doctor but we never forgot the incompetence of that nurse. 'She should have known better.'"

"I stayed in the hospital for twelve days because of infection. At that time, nine days was considered normal for child delivery. Earl and I named him William after William Zeidel, a dear friend who lived in Cleveland, Ohio. His middle name was Gary. He stayed in the hospital another six weeks before we could bring him home. The doctor instructed us to carry him on a silk pillow. Billy started to eat right away and never lost an ounce of weight. Earl and Betty, my oldest daughter, went to the hospital every day to see the baby. When he came home he had gained a pound. He weighed 3 pounds and one ounce. In spite of all the troubles we went through to get Billy here, he was never sick once during the first three and a half years. Everyone called him, 'Billy'."

"The day Billy was born, the head day nurse gave Earl a bill for the delivery room for forty-three dollars. Earl told the nurse, 'My wife never used the delivery room or had any help in delivery.' The nurse on duty that day said she was unaware of the trouble but subtracted the fee from the bill."

"We stayed in the Ravenna house where the accident happened for six months, until Earl contracted TNT poisoning. This required extended treatment during which time he went to Painesville to work. But, trouble was no stranger to our family."

Bill's baby picture

A Functional Alcoholic

EARL Reid recalled, "Billy was our ninth child. The oldest was Betty Sue, followed by John, George, and Raymond (who died as an infant), Allen, Barbara, Dorothy, Louis, and Billy. Donald came along after Billy and caught the worst of Billy's jealousy and meanness. Ruth followed Donald as the youngest."

"I was 38 years old when Billy was born. I was born in 1907 on September 22. I thought of myself as a typical working class man. I was married. I had kids and worked long hours wherever I could find work. I never was a slacker! Most of my early work was painting houses. I painted until the war came along in 1940. When World War II started I was past the draft age. Besides, I had a family of ten to support. There was better money in factory work during the war. Climbing and painting was pretty hard work so I took a factory job in an arsenal in Ravenna making war materials. Later, after Billy was born I moved to a chemical factory in Painesville."

"The pay was good. The hours were long. Like most men around I spent most of my waking hours in the factory. We worked swing shifts. We would work days; be off two days and work nights. Weekends were spent running family errands and visiting friends in the local bars." Earl's heavy drinking caused family members to remember him in later years as a "functional alcoholic".

"No, I wasn't very religious. I didn't go to church but Esther and I agreed to have the children baptized as babies. Sundays, Esther and the kids loaded in the family car and went to church unless the kids were sick or hurt, which was much of the time. I just wasn't the social type. I usually stopped off at one of the bars on my way home from work to let off a little steam. I don't think I drank too much."

The Reid family remembers there always seemed to be a half empty bottle around the house. Earl's drinking habits were picked up by some of his sons as they grew older.

Earl was handy with his hands and in later years built two houses for his family. In his way he cared for his family the way generations of hard-working fathers had done. He was long on hard work but short on affection. His rule was to give each child the same attention, believing in the old adage that all children should be treated alike. It sounded fair but in reality no two children were alike. Needs varied from child to child. Had Earl recognized this things might have been different for his ninth child, Billy….and this book would never have been written...had his kids been treated individually.

"When Billy came along, things changed. He needed more care and Esther had to stay home with him. On top of that, John, our second child had been in a serious accident and spent years in and out of hospitals. Between trips to hospitals and doctors and taking care of Billy's special need, things were different. As Billy grew older we had more trouble trying to manage him. We couldn't take him too many public places without an ordeal. No matter how much we tried to show Billy we loved him, he stayed frustrated with his limitations and learning disabilities. Billy never bonded with me and Esther. He just got more and more frustrated. At times he was just plain violent toward the younger kids."

Earl contracted TNT poisoning working at the arsenal. Prolonged exposure to TNT resulted in a discoloration of both skin and hair, a symptom that led years later to a Public Broadcasting Series entitled, **The Girls with Yellow Hands.** It focused on female munitions workers in Britain during World War I. Aside from the obvious danger of explosion and long working hours in munitions factories, workers faced this more insidious danger of long-term exposure to trinitrotoluene, commonly known as TNT. Additional symptoms of TNT poisoning included headaches, vomiting, nausea and cold-like symptoms. Before the yellowing of the skin and headaches became apparent, the longer lasting, more dangerous effects from handling TNT had already taken their toll on Earl Reid. Several months of recuperation followed his poisoning. After his recovery he went to Painesville to work at Diamond Shamrock, a chemical factory.

"Before Billy was born, we were already trying to deal with an accident that happened to John, our second-born. He was accidentally struck by an automobile on the highway near our house. Because of the accident John spent seven years in and out of hospitals in Ohio.

A Family Crisis

JOHN, the second child in the Reid family, was born on March 12, 1931 on a cold day near Geneva. Ohio on the Lake. The family lived in the township. Betty, the oldest child, was born two years earlier on December 29, 1929. Both births took place at home.

On Election Day, November 8, 1938, eight year old John was looking forward to celebrating Thanksgiving. He and his classmates were making decorations at school. Esther told John not to forget to get a haircut that afternoon.

John recalled the afternoon clearly years later. "I was wearing my heavy winter coat and walking across West Main Street. I got across the street and remembered I was to go to my uncle's barber shop for a haircut. I cut back across the street diagonally like I had seen others do. I don't remember what happened next. A young woman in a car ran the red light, hit me and dragged me forty feet. I believe I was on the curb when I was hit. The woman in the car veered and hit me on my right side."

"My older sister, Betty, was crossing the railroad tracks when someone told her that I had been hit by a car. She asked if I had died and the kid told her that he didn't know. She ran home to find a strange car in the driveway and her Mother crying. The car took Esther to the hospital. "I don't know how long I was unconscious but I remember waking up in the back seat of a car. I was crying and there was a lot of blood in the car."

"A Mrs. Heidelman was driving by and saw the accident. She loaded me into her back seat and took me to the hospital. I remember being wheeled to the operating room. I was crying and there was blood everywhere. My Mom and Dad got there later. I remember seeing them standing at the doorway. I told them the light was red. I kept repeating it, until I went into a coma."

"Dr. Hutchinson, the family doctor, came out of the operating room and told my parents I probably wouldn't live. My skull was fractured. My Dad fired that doctor and hired a Dr. Burroughs from Ashtabula who cleaned me up. My leg was broken in nine places. The doctor took his hands and squeezed the bones of my leg back together. My next recollection was waking up in a room with my Dad sitting in a rocking chair."

"I was in the hospital almost a year. I got out in August 1939. In December I was cleaning snow off the porch and slipped breaking and dislocating my right elbow. Two doctors reset my elbow and put it in a cast. When it healed my arm was set crooked. It was twisted around. I couldn't do much with it and had to walk on my toes due to my earlier accident. Things really became difficult for me. My right leg was a half inch longer than the left due to the accident."

"They told my parents I would never walk again. I came home happy to be on crutches. The following September I was out on the porch holding our dog by a leash and the dog took off and I ended on the sidewalk with a dislocated elbow which was broken. The doctor put me to sleep in his office and put my arm in a cast. I probably had osteoporosis because of poor eating habits."

"That fall or winter I was chasing George or he was chasing me and I slipped, fell, broke and dislocated my elbow again. Mom took me to the doctor and he recommended I go to Gates Hospital in Elyria where crippled children were treated. They ex-rayed me from head to toe. Dr. Hyman recommended they straighten my elbow and fuse my right foot to keep me from walking on my toes. In November I went into the hospital and had the operation. In early December 1941 I came home on Sunday, the day Pearl Harbor was attacked. 'Be quiet,' my Dad yelled. 'Shut up so I can hear the news.' I don't remember much about the talk between Mom and Dad but the whole country was at war. My Dad was working in the defense factory in Wadsworth. In January they removed the cast from my elbow and leg so I could use both."

"In late summer 1941 I was playing football across the street from where we lived. In spite of all my injuries and surgeries, Dad and Mom treated me like the rest of the kids and allowed me to play just as rough as they did. A kid tackled me and knocked me down. I had a terrible pain in my right leg. It hurt so bad! In a few days it stopped hurting. A few days later, my leg suddenly swelled like a tumor and the doctor decided to lance it in his office. I ended up back in Kid's Hospital. I had osteonueritis, an infection that eats the bone. That's how one of my legs became shorter than the other. I was in the hospital this time for eleven months. They had sides on the bed but I got out of bed and broke the right femur again. The doctors had me strapped down so I couldn't raise up."

"It was a boy's ward and they treated us well. Dr. Herndon, Dr. Hyman, and a local Doctor, Dr. Lawrence, called on me. They changed the dressings. There were about 14 boys in the same shape I was in. I was in the front of the hospital facing the street. My friends from school would come and stand in the snow and wave to me. I had a bandage on my head and my leg was in traction straight up."

"Mom and Dad couldn't visit often. Dad had moved to Shaylersville out in the country with no electricity. They had to cook on a wood stove and pump water. They had a garden. Mom did most of the gardening."

"Dr. Burroughs transferred me to Ashtabula General. When they lowered my leg I started screaming. In the end they gave me two blood transfusions. They placed me in a sun room where I stayed for months with my leg in traction. They would take it down only to ex-ray me. I had a twenty-five pound weight on my spine and one on my leg. I laid there and waved to people who came by. My Aunt would come and give me candy and gum. Mom and Dad would come periodically from Geneva which was 10 miles away."

"I don't remember much about those days in the hospital. I have fond memories of growing up with Betty, George, Barbara, (one infant death), and Allen. We took lumps of dirt from neighbor's gardens and threw them in the street. One day I threw a rock and a car was coming. The rock went through the vent on the car and knocked the guy's glasses off. He came to the door and we hid under the bed. Mom pulled us out and made us apologize. I was very young then."

"The Nickel Plate Railroad ran through Geneva and the New York Central, too. There were lots of passengers. There were also bums and tramps. My folks said there was a difference between a bum and a tramp. They would stop for something to eat. Dad was a painter and truck driver and had sailed on the Great Lakes. In the early thirties he was sailing the lakes but drove trucks later on. We moved down to Cherryville and he worked at the arsenal there."

"We moved again into a duplex in Geneva for a while. George and I were lighting matches in the house and throwing them behind a mirror in the house. We got spanked for it. In 1936-1937 there was a ball diamond across the street and the circus would come there."

"Dad was having a problem drinking. He was painting houses at the time. Those years between 1939 and 1941 were hard times. Dad got a job in Cleveland. George and I would go into the fields and eat raw corn. We would camp out near the Cuyahoga river. We would take food from home to camp out. We didn't realize how tough it was in those days. Those were the days of the great depression. Then one afternoon in November, George and I were in a baby buggy going down a steep hill. My sister was in the front part and I went over her and hit the ground. She heard the bone snap. I broke the femur again."

"That was the third time it broke and back into Gates hospital I went. I lost weight. I didn't want to eat. The return of the infection was a common symptom but doctors were afraid it had moved to my hip. I was there several months until it healed. They did surgery to graft skin to my heel. That was in 1942-1944. My heel had been eaten away by the cast from the four surgeries in seven months. They made a tube out of my skin and sewed it to my heel. I had hair growing on my heel for a long time. When the cast was taken off, one foot was glued to the calf of my leg until it healed. I had to learn to walk again which happened nearly every time I was operated on."

"Mom and Dad moved to Charden Township. Dad went to work for Diamond Shamrock. We raised chickens, ducks and rabbits on the farm. George and I would hunt with Dad for squirrels. We would go out on our own. This was in the 1934-36 time. Dad bought a farm with about 60 acres later on."

"In Charden, I was playing baseball with the kids and running to first base when my knee cap popped off to one side. Dad had both kneecaps broken by a cow as a child and he knew what was going on. It was a hereditary thing. Both my great grandparents had weakness in their knees. Not all members in the family were affected but some of us were. I went back to the hospital to have knee surgery. Mine turned out to be the first successful operation to stabilize a kneecap. I was there for months and had to learn to walk again. I had to learn to walk again seven separate times from all the broken bones and surgeries."

"I had so many surgeries that I had a phobia the rest of my life whenever my face was covered. I had a big scar caused by the lime in the cast eating away the back of my leg. They cured my staph infection with sulfa drug. My uncle knew someone who had it flown in. This was in 1938. It was hard to get. That saved my life. I came home in August. In the meantime, Allen was born and a baby when I got home."

"I remember my Mom's visits. Transportation was a problem. Dad would stay outside with the kids. I came very close to death with that infection. They saved my life. Coming home to my family was different. I had to learn to walk again. I was determined to walk. Doctors said I would not walk again. My right leg was a half inch longer due to the healing process. I had braces and a lift. I spent close to five years in the hospitals from 1938 to 1946."

"Dad and Mom never complained about the depression. We didn't know it was a depression. Mom and Dad would walk out of the grocery with two big bags of food. Mom put up with a lot. Dad would get up in the middle of the night and stop at the tavern. He would stop there on the way home. He would walk two miles through Ohio snows to get to the tavern. Mother worked all the time."

"Billy was born March 24, 1943. He was born at Robinson Memorial Hospital in Geneva. He weighed only three pounds and two ounces when my parents brought him home. My brother Donald was born in 1945 in Shelby. Ruth Ann was born in 1951 in Cleveland in St. Luke hospital." After Billy was born he would cry and hold his breath until he turned blue and Mom would have to shake him and stop him from doing it. She had a hard time."

"We just took life in stride and went on. We would gather scrap and sell it to the Junk man for eleven cents. It cost a dime to go to a movie and one cent for candy. It was living. My Dad had strokes later in life and Mom had to take care of him. Life was good for us kids in spite of the troubles. I never knew what was happening to Billy at State School or how it affected him until after he had gotten out and changed."

John survived the accident but was badly crippled in both legs. His right leg had been crushed below the knee. The bone above the knee was displaced a full inch and a half. He also suffered a severe cut above his left eye. The osteoporosis that infected his wounds was treated with the new miracle drug (it was 1938) called sulfa. Dr. Clarence Hindman, a noted orthopedic surgeon was called to help treat John's injuries. The results were truly amazing to both parents. John recovered enough to earn a living for him and was old enough that he was not as affected by Billy's problems when he was born.

The two youngest children, Donald and Ruth, were another story. Because Donald was born two years after Billy, and developed as a normal child, he became the focus of Billy's frustration and growing rage over his own disabilities. There were constant fights between the two brothers. The difference Billy lacked in size and strength in those battles was more than compensated for by his extreme anger. Years later, both Donald and Billy recalled many of the fights from their childhood. Billy vividly remembered wanting to kill Donald and other family members. John recalled, "When Billy went to State School we didn't know what was going on. I remember visiting him and he never complained. I've heard him talk since about what God has done for him but at the time I was unaware of any of those things."

Born for Trouble

BILLY was Earl and Esther's ninth child. After his miraculous pre-mature birth the doctor cautioned Esther not to allow the baby to catch a cold or be exposed to illness. She was instructed to carry him on a pillow and handle him as little as possible to prevent any injury. Billy began to eat and had a good appetite. Because of his premature birth and undetermined injuries he didn't walk before he was three years old nor did his first teeth appear until after he was a year old. Esther and Earl took their tiny son to the family doctor to find the cause of his impaired growth. The doctor could detect nothing to explain Billy's inability to walk. His sister, Betty, would place Billy's feet on her feet in an attempt to teach him to walk. He simply could not stand alone. Two years later his younger brother, Donald, was born. He weighed more than nine pounds at birth.

Donald progressed rapidly. When Billy was three his brother was walking, but Billy could not walk. Esther took Billy to the local doctor but his examination revealed nothing out of the ordinary. He simply couldn't stand. Donald began to talk but Billy was not talking. Esther found a walker for Billy which he propelled around the house without any difficulty, but he did not walk. The walker was taken away, but still he would not attempt to stand or walk. The doctor examined him again but found nothing wrong. Billy looked healthy.

Other measures were taken. Family members took turns placing Billy's feet on their feet and walking with him. His balance remained unsteady. When he could stand and take a few steps, any irregularity in the floor would cause him to fall.

At age four the Reids approached Dr. Hindman who had done wonders for John, the older son, in his accident. "Would he agree to see Billy," they asked? An appointment was made and Dr. Hindman examined four-year-old Billy. The physical examination seemed rough to Esther and Earl who continued to treat Billy as a frail child. His opinion was that the fall in the pregnancy had caused nerve damage to Billy that affected both his balance and his eyesight. He was four years of age then. The doctor offered no further treatment. "Nothing can be done, " he told them. His diagnosis was that the nerves in the back of his neck were crossed. Any surgery would have to take place at age seven. They were to bring Billy back every four months for check-ups.

Billy continued to fall frequently. Someone in the family had to be with him all the time. Playing outdoors left him with numerous cuts and bruises. His brother, Donald, was growing normally. He ate well, played well, and grew. Billy could not eat well. He was messy when he tried to eat. He appeared to be left handed but at times favored his right hand. Donald was left-handed. Donald would help Billy walk, but Billy would become frustrated because he could not do what Donald did. All of the children were very protective of Billy. Esther dressed Billy and Donald alike hoping to erase some of the growing differences between the two boys.

Earl and Esther tried not to make distinctions between Billy and Donald but the differences were there. Both parents and family members referred to him as "Billy" and Donald became known as "Don." Because of his slow development everyone treated Billy like a small child. All the while he grew mentally but was unable to communicate his growing frustrations in a positive manner.

Another doctor was consulted in 1946. Dr. Green worked as an osteopath. He worked with Billy's coordination and joint movement. Most of the time family members carried Billy. It was easier than letting him walk. Dr. Green instructed the family to make a swing to help him build strength in his legs and arms. The therapy worked and Billy was able to walk, although with noticeable difficulty. Dr. Hindman was pleased with the results. He was reluctant to operate on Billy. The surgery would have been very "tricky." The decision was made to let him alone and enroll him in school.

Billy was seven years old when he started to school. Donald was already in school learning to read and write. Billy couldn't read or write. Seeing his younger brother do things he could not do frustrated him more. He became increasingly agitated by his younger brother's progress and his own inabilities. Mrs. Hammer, his teacher in the first and second grades, was unable to cope with him. Billy seemed to have a good mind but his hands and mind did not appear to work together. He simply couldn't grasp the purpose of school.

If he had gone to school orally Billy probably would have done well, but he could not concentrate on instruction. He continually looked around the room to see what others were doing. Donald was a good student but Billy picked up the work of other children and scrawled his own name on their papers. He attempted to copy their answers. Classroom discipline in the early forties was meted out in spanking. Mrs. Hammer spanked Billy daily! Reports of his misconduct reached home and were duly rewarded with more spankings with the big leather belt reserved for all the children by his mother. None of this stopped him from throwing things in the classroom or being disruptive in dozens of ways.

The Reids decided to take Billy to Dr. Hindman for another opinion. The doctor's advice was to ignore Billy's wrong behavior. This had an adverse effect on Donald. He started to withdraw into a shell. He didn't bring any school work home. If Billy was in the room he would not talk about his work. He would wait until Billy was out of hearing before talking about his school work. He did not want to say that Billy couldn't do the same things. Esther continued to dress the two boys identically as twins.

Dr. Hindman, advised the Reids to take Billy to a psychiatrist who specialized in young children. The doctor told them that Billy's IQ was about 70 which was below average but suggested that an oral exam might indicate a higher score. Orally, Billy could answer questions although with difficulty. The doctor's opinion was that Donald and Billy should be separated at school.

Without Donald to run interference the teacher simply gave up on Billy. She confessed that she simply didn't know how to teach him. His brothers and sisters were unable to teach him to read or write. He remained in the first grade for two years and the second grade for two more years. By the time he reached the third grade his habit of taking school work belonging to other children had become so frequent that he disrupted class. He began crying in school.

Whenever anyone corrected him Billy would hold his breath until he turned blue. It scared his family and his teachers. The doctor admitted that Billy was smart in a cunning way. He could get the attention he craved. At home family members left him alone and he would stop the behavior after a while. When he did resort to holding his breath they would pick him up, slap him on the back and force air into his lungs.

Billy resorted to other tactics. He delighted tripping children in the classroom as they came out of the room. The children cried. The teacher cried. She really tried to reach Billy but simply could not make him understand. Her last resort was written to the parents. "I cannot put up with Billy any longer. He has hurt too many children and disrupted classes too often."

Dr. Hindman set up an appointment with a psychiatrist from Kent State University. Billy was examined for an hour. He sent Billy to an outside office while he talked with his mother. The doctor had a two-way mirror and could see Billy listening at the door to his explanations. He stepped into an inner room and told Billy's parents to take him out of school and think about Donald. They gave Billy a label. He was "spastic". He had a good IQ but he was cunning. He didn't belong in an institution for the retarded. He was too smart for that.

The doctor advised the Reids to think about Donald. Billy didn't care what happened to Donald. He had to be removed from school. At home Billy's eyes and face were unable to hide the anger and rage he felt toward his younger brother, Donald, or his other siblings. Donald was unable to cope with school, especially with Billy's disabilities. The doctor's advice was to place Billy with a foster home that specialized in children like him. He contacted the Charden Health Department who found a family in Cincinnati who agreed to help. There were no other children in the home. It was not an adoption but a state sponsored arrangement. When it came time for Billy to go there, the woman in the home had a heart attack and foster adoption was ruled out.

When his younger brother, Donald, was moved to grade three, Billy was promoted with him. Although he could not read or write the opinion was that with Donald he might begin to learn. Mrs. Clasp, his third grade teacher could do nothing with him. Bill remembered her in later years as a sweet and kind person but she could not deal with the angry child in her room. Billy was convinced everyone was picking on him. Any attempt to teach or instruct him caused him to react with anger. He picked up whatever was convenient and used it as a weapon. He never considered the consequences. The decision was made by the school to permanently expel him from school. After Billy left school his third grade teacher, Mrs. Clasp, died of a heart attack. Some in the community blamed Billy's tantrums for causing the fatal attack. It may be hard to believe that a ten year-old child could cause such problems, but it happened.

The fights continued at home. Since he was the older boy, Billy felt he had to win every argument and every fight. His memory of those fights with his brother and neighboring children was that he meant to hurt whomever he fought. Earl Reid's response was simply to yell for him to stop. Billy was angry at his father but didn't know why.

There were sixty acres with their house. During the years Billy was confined to home between the ages of ten and thirteen he spent much of his free time roaming over those acres and in the surrounding area. He broke into homes while the owners were at work or school. He stole anything of interest to a small boy, including money. He stole from his father and mother's wallets when he had the opportunity. He discovered the effect of alcohol. His father kept a ready supply for his own use and made beer for his own consumption. Many of the neighbors made beer and kept alcohol in their homes. Billy drank whatever he found.

During the summer months Billy and Donald often spent nights in tents in the back yard. The boys would roam the neighborhood after their parents went to bed. They shared their beer, cigarettes and whiskey with other kids in the neighborhood. They amused themselves by placing debris in the road past their house at night. When drivers stopped they ran into the nearby corn field to hide.

As Billy grew older he and Donald visited the bar where their father went and sold empty bottles. Everyone in the area knew the Reid kids. Visits to the local dance hall gave opportunity to steal cigarettes. Ziglar's Place, the bar their father frequented, had an open field behind it where older kids raced cars on an improvised dirt track. The young brothers either watched or hitched rides to the nearby town of Charden where they slipped into the movie theatre. Billy was the thief and chief instigator of trouble. The boys stole fruits and vegetables in the summer months from their neighbors. They brought them home with the story that neighbors had given them. Nights they often slipped out an upstairs window and down a fire ladder escape. Esther related years later that she stayed up nights waiting for them to return home. Billy was living up to the prediction that he was born for trouble.

Call Me Bill!

As Billy grew older he began to follow an older brother, Allen, to work on a nearby farm. The owners of the farm took an interest in Billy and taught him to do things his own parents never allowed, including driving the farm tractor. They complimented him and told him he was smart. They said, "You can learn to do anything." Others called him "stupid" and "dumb." It seemed he could not learn the elementary basics of reading and writing. Had he been born a generation later, he most probably would have been diagnosed with dyslexia and taught how to overcome the disability but this was the early fifties. Allen's employers were like second parents to Billy. He even stayed nights with them at times.

A county nurse was sent to the Reid's home periodically to give Billy necessary shots for immunizations. Mrs. Landin, the nurse, had Billy's records with her when she arrived. She knew Billy had begun to hurt people. His violence made his younger brother, Donald, more aggressive, too. Six years after Billy's birth, Ruth was born. By the time she reached two years of age Billy had become violently resentful of her, also. Not only did he threaten Ruth and Donald but he threatened the older children as well.

By this time Billy had developed a fascination with fire. He would burn matches in the house and on one occasion set a fire in his room pretending that he was camping outdoors. Fortunately, he had invited the family dog to the bedroom weiner roast who started to bark. The barking alerted Mrs. Reid who came running and screamed for him to put out the fire. Billy had no concept of danger or the consequences of his actions. The entire family watched him constantly.

Donald and Billy were playing in an empty chicken house behind their home one afternoon when Billy set fire to the building. Donald was inside when the fire was set. There was some fear that Billy knew what he was doing when he lighted the fire. Donald escaped unharmed but the threat to the family increased.

Earl loved his troubled son. He called him Uncle Bill after Ruth's birth but his long hours of work on a swing shift and heavy use of alcohol left little time for Billy along with the demands of ten other children. Billy's behavior worsened.

From age ten to thirteen Billy's behavior grew worse. He was smaller than other children his age and a target for larger children. Any sign of bullying or teasing was met with anger. There were repeated episodes of violence and anger. Things reached a crisis one afternoon when the family dog began to howl in an upstairs room. Billy was in the room with his nephew and younger sister, Ruth. When Esther opened the door she found Billy with an iron rail raised over his head ready to hit the younger children. They were playing with their backs to him, unaware of the threat. Esther grabbed him and shook him. "Billy you get downstairs!" She didn't tell the little ones what she had seen. Instead, Billy went into a back room. Tears streamed down Esther's face as she confronted the angry little boy. "Why did you do that," she cried? Billy shrugged. "What's going to happen," he asked?

Mrs. Reid called the county nurse, Mrs. Landin, and told her something had to be done. She really scolded Billy for his behavior. He simply stood looking at her and shrugged his shoulders. Esther told the nurse, "If something isn't done I'm going to have a stroke or heart attack. I can't carry this any longer. His Dad doesn't know all he does. I can't bring myself to tell him everything."

Three days later one of the older boys, Lewis, found two tools under Billy's mattress belonging to his father---a large steel wrench and a butcher knife. "What did he intend to do with those things?" Esther's mind raced. "Would he get up some night and hurt someone?" The nurse went to the judge at Chardon and showed him Billy's records. There was a placement waiting list of nine children ahead of Billy. The judge didn't feel he could place Billy before any of them.

Two days later the judge asked to see Billy and Esther. He had a psychiatrist with him whom Esther had not met. They took Billy's clothing off and stood him in front of them in his underclothing. They looked him over and examined him. The doctor examined Billy and handed him sheets of paper with blots of ink on them (most probably a Rorschach test). When he asked Billy to describe his feelings about the ink blots Billy responded each time with answers like: "I see an explosion." The doctor and judge explained, "Mrs. Reid you'd be surprised how many children we have to put in school with broken bones from bad homes. Billy has no bruises. He has some scars from falls as a child but nothing more. He needs supervision and training. I'll set it up for Billy to leave home." It was October when the judge made the decision.

Billy was sent away from home in November. He was thirteen years old. His older sister, Betty, who was now married and a mother of three, drove Esther and Billy to Columbus, Ohio to the State School for children. There seemed to be no other option open to the family. The parting was painful and difficult for his mother and sister. Billy showed no emotion in the separation. His anger and bitterness were locked within him. The admitting nurse intended to interview the family when they took Billy inside. Billy spoke to her and said, "I want to be called Bill, not Billy." That's all Betty remembered hearing him say. "Call me Bill." She did remember the burning hatred in Billy's eyes when he realized he was being left behind. They left him there before Thanksgiving. After a full year he was allowed a visit home at Christmas where he stayed for a week and a half. He came home for a few vacations in the summer. Most of the children in the school were not allowed this privilege.

Billy with Father

Billy with Father and Mother

Billy with Mother on Bench

State School

O N April 17, 1857, the State of Ohio established the Ohio Asylum for the Education of Idiotic and Imbecile Youth. During its history, the organization went through several name changes, including the Institution for the Education of Idiotic and Imbecile Youth (1878-1881), the Institution for Feeble-Minded Youth (1881-1945), the Columbus State School (1945-1970), the Columbus State Institute (1970-1980), and the Columbus Developmental Center (1980-present). It was commonly referred to as the Institution for Feeble-Minded Youth and by its shorter name, State School. In the beginning the institution rented several buildings on East Main Street in Columbus, Ohio. In the first year of the Institution for Feeble-Minded Youth's existence, nine students enrolled. By the third year, the institution began to average between forty and fifty students every year.[1]

Institution for Feeble Minded, Columbus. O.

State School

Due to the institution's success, the Ohio legislature authorized the construction of an actual campus for the school on East Broad Street.[2] Completed in 1868, the institution soon enrolled more than three hundred students. On November 18, 1881, a fire struck the school, destroying several of the buildings. The six hundred students escaped unharmed. The Institution for Feeble-Minded Youth rebuilt the destroyed buildings and enrollment skyrocketed to 1,100 students in 1900. Eventually, other branches were opened across Ohio.

The Institution for Feeble-Minded Youth enrolled both boys and girls, children who struggled in public schools of their own communities. The intent was for the institution to give the children a chance to enroll in a more supervised and stringent setting. The Institution for Feeble-Minded Youth also provided the children with vocational training, with the boys working on a farm owned by the school and the girls performing domestic duties. The intent was to help students with various learning and social problems and develop the skills necessary to lead productive lives.

Billy's older sister, Betty, would not leave her small children alone with him on any of his infrequent visits home. She was terrified what Billy might do to one of them if left alone with them. Billy was reminded more than once that he was born for trouble.

Billy was confined to the school in the Fall of the year. He was just thirteen years old. Confinement is the proper word because the school campus was surrounded by fencing. Even if he dared escape the fence he knew no one in Columbus and had no knowledge how to travel alone.

The first Christmas came and passed alone in State School. He was required to stay at least one year before being given a week and a half furlough. Brief visits home were allowed at Christmas and for a week in summer. Some Christmas seasons no one from the Reid family was able to come to Columbus to escort Billy home. Those years he spent at State School. In his brief visits he continued to create trouble. His brothers and sisters were growing up, associating with friends while Billy had no friends. The anger he was forced to internalize at school would erupt at home. In effect, he had no family.

He was escorted home and back to school by his mother who travelled by bus or train from Painesville to Columbus and back.

Billy later related that some attendants were kind to the kids but others were not so kind. A few workers took advantage of those who were trying to work their way out of State School. They were nice to them and invited them to visit in their homes. This was absolutely forbidden by the school both for the workers and the kids. Some of the workers would have residents come and cut grass and clean house and do odd jobs. A few of these workers were caught and fired by the school.

Wanting to make as many good points as possible, residents were always willing to accept these invitations. If questioned about it, everyone denied it; the workers and the residents. If questioned about another kid, everyone denied knowing anything for fear of creating problems for themselves with the School or the attendants.

Billy said, "The workers would tell us, 'Don't say anything. Just come over to my house and wash my windows. If you say anything about this, you'll get into trouble.' I knew if I said anything about anyone else I would get the boy in trouble and me in trouble for saying it. This went on quite a bit. These residents were trying to work their way out. We were told, 'If you ever get a job, you can never get a state job. You belong to the state. You don't belong to your parents anymore because your parents don't pay for your stay here. The state pays your expenses.' My parents might send me five dollars a year because they didn't have much money, so I believed the state workers. I was led to believe that parents had been told that this kid doesn't belong to you anymore. He belongs to the state. You have no more say about him. We were told, 'You have to do what we tell you whether you like it or not. You belong to us. You will never get out of here.'"

In 1945 State Schools began admitting children under five years of age. This was seen at the time as progress and a help to parents of severely disabled children. If the same criteria employed at Willowbrook State School in New York were used in Columbus, limited numbers of infants could begin to be admitted. Edith Stern, a reporter of that era, wrote several articles on the topic of children with disabilities. Her article written in the August, 1948 edition of **Women's Home Companion** was entitled "Take them Off the Human Scrap Heap." Numerous descriptions were offered of deplorable conditions similar to those made famous by Geraldo Rivera in his exposé of Willowbrook State School some twenty-five years later. Articles about these conditions and the resulting incidents of death or ill-fated escapes appeared in the newspapers and were known to the public who for the most part remained indifferent.[3]

For sure, the conditions described were true for Billy Reid. He was not mentally retarded. He knew what was happening to him. Regardless of his emotional frustration and anger issues, he had a perfectly good mind to process the fact that he was being placed on "the human scrap heap." Little wonder that his inner turmoil and rage continued to grow as he endured the abuse and confinement at Columbus State School.

The public began to recognize the field of mental retardation was at a very low point, suffering from scientific pessimism and neglect (the dominant psychiatric view that mental retardation was permanent and incurable), lacking trained personnel and facilities, isolated from other human services, and a growing reputation of hopelessness."

As someone who lived in and survived an institution that was not equipped for and lacked the accountability to properly care for disturbed children, what weighed heavily on Bill after he was set free was the children he saw who simply shouldn't have been there — that is, children who were "institutionalized," not based on disability, but based on what could only be explained as a misunderstanding and misdiagnosis of their disabilities by stressed parents, mental health physicians, caregivers — and a system that supported such poor treatment.

Not all care facilities were bad. Many people required long-term, skilled care for their disabilities. Loving parents and care givers were unable to care for all of these. Having such facilities ensured the health and well-being of those affected when properly administered.

Columbus State School occupied a ten block square from North Broad Street in Columbus, Ohio to Sullivan Street. It was west of downtown, fenced to keep residents within the several dormitories and classrooms. The school had a guard staff and was assisted by the city police department who patrolled the area.

Dormitories were referred to as "areas" where residents with similar physical and emotional needs were housed. Dormitories housed between thirty and thirty-five residents at a time. Age was not the qualifying condition of each dormitory. Girls and young women were housed in separate areas from male residents.

Four attendants were assigned each dormitory in the daytime but nights usually had only one attendant on duty. Attendants routinely left the dormitories with their residents in the charge of older residents within the area. These residents had no training for their assignments and needed special care themselves. At times, three to six of these older residents would select a younger, weaker resident and teach him a lesson. One would keep watch for the absent attendant while the others took the resident into a shower room and beat him or sexually assaulted him.

If a victim reported the incident to an attendant it was written up but nothing ever done about it. Instead, the victims were given more severe beatings by the older residents to shut them up. They were also told not to tell their parents or visitors of such incidents lest they find out and further beatings occur. Most residents learned not to speak out.

CDC was not home nor was it designed to be home. Many residents had no contact with family or friends. The only family they had was the residents and staff. Some did not attempt to escape because they were from distant communities, young, and with no way of surviving in a strange city.

A few residents received gifts from home; cookies, five dollars once a year. Money was exchanged by the staff for a card bearing the amount held by the school. Residents often used the cookies and money to bribe older students not to mistreat them or buy smokes if their parents had given them permission with the school.

A mess hall was located near each dormitory. Residents ate their meals within the mess hall. In the case of severely handicapped residents, learning to feed themselves was one of the goals of the staff. Residents who wanted to find a way out of State School sometimes volunteered to feed the severely handicapped.

Classrooms or instruction rooms were also located near each dormitory area. Residents were taught basic skills that might be used on the outside to support themselves. The instruction included dishwashing, mopping, sweeping, shoe repair, and assisting the more physically impaired residents in their basic needs.

Once a resident learned to follow instruction and perform basic skills it was possible to move to a dormitory with more advanced training in these trades. For those who were able to "move up" to an advanced dormitory, life became easier but the beatings and rapes continued for the weaker among them.

Residents lived with fear. There were threats and intimidation. The goal of the older residents and the attendants was control. The staff warned the residents unless they learned to listen and follow instruction they would never leave the school. The stronger of the residents told the weaker ones that they were under their control and no one could help them. Both were true statements.

Bill Reid quickly learned to listen to his instructors and master some skills usable on the outside. By age sixteen, he had moved to a less threatening dormitory area where the abuse he had experienced was less frequent.

Bill related in later years, "If it was not for God's grace and love, I don't know how I would ever have gotten through it. I wanted to give up. I had so much hate in me for what my family and others had done to me. I might easily have been left in that place for the rest of my life."

Although changes in the treatment of handicapped persons has improved over time, parents and caregivers who are unable to meet the needs of the handicapped in their care should make careful observation and periodic visits to institutions before committing a person to its care.

House of Horror

BILL Reid remembered his arrival at State School vividly. It was 1956. "I was thirteen years old. An instructor told me to pick up a mop and start cleaning. I had developed an attitude at home and school never to take anything off anybody. I turned and walked away. The instructor picked up a broom and hit me in the head. 'You want to be tough? I'll show you what tough is.' Another instructor told me I might as well listen because I would never leave this place. My parents had abandoned me, given me up."

"I lost all hope in my family and everyone I had ever known. I knew I couldn't get along with my family. Now, I had no one to care for me. I had nothing but hate in me."

The next eight years of Bill's life were spent primarily behind walls and fences among mentally and emotionally handicapped residents. Years later this institution would be converted to house the criminally insane. The abuse he suffered from his first day there until he was twenty-one years of age only fueled his frustration and rage.

Billy was assigned to a dormitory and a bed. There were thirty to forty assigned to the room. They ranged in age from six years of age to fifty, all in the same room.

Two attendants were assigned in the daytime but only one at night. The first night Billy was beaten up by three or four of the older residents. "The purpose of those beatings was to establish control over you. The worse abuse took place at night. The night attendant would take a head count of the room every two hours but between counts he would go into his office and stay there until time to check beds."

"Lights were turned out for the smaller children at eight o'clock. Older residents were required to be in bed by ten o'clock. When lights were out it was time to find out how tough you were. Older residents would slap new arrivals to see if they would fight back. I was a fighter but I had to quit fighting because I was too little and kept getting beaten up."

"Beatings were not the worst part. The older ones would gag me and choke me to keep me from screaming, strip off my clothes, and force me to 'do sexual things.' Although 'rape' was never said, younger and weaker residents were systematically raped by older residents. We were warned if we told anyone what happened, we would be beaten again. One kid would watch through a window for the attendant while the other kids came in one by one and beat you up or abused you. I was confined in that place the first two of my teenage years until I managed to move up to another dormitory."

"A few kids reported their abuse. The older kids beat them up when they got them alone. Nothing was done about it. Smaller kids were taken to the bathroom where their heads were pushed into a toilet and the toilet flushed. They were told by the older ones, 'You're mine and you can't do anything about it!' They were stronger. I learned not to tell."

"Once in a while a kid ran away. When he was caught and brought back, he was placed in a small room by the attendant. The room had no ventilation. The heat was unbearable. A can was left in the room for a toilet. A runaway would be there for one or two weeks in only his underwear. Other kids would make fun of the one confined. I was beat up several times and I beat up a few, too."

"There were rumors of two kids being killed. I don't know how they were killed. One guard was killed. I went to the funeral of the one who died. There were some suicides but no one talked about it. You were always under pressure and afraid. I was beat up the first night I was there. Nights, I didn't go to sleep until everyone else went to sleep. Some nights attendants would take you to a back room, lock you in there and beat you because you didn't listen to what they told you to do."

"We rarely had any contact with girls. There were girls on the same campus. The school had a dance once each week. There were four girls' dorms. Each dormitory had thirty girls. They were anywhere from six years of age through their twenties. They were all messed up. I was thirteen when I got there. When the girls got you into a bedroom, they would do whatever they wanted."

"We were allowed to play only in certain areas outside the dorms. A religious service was held once a week. Someone would come and preach. All I remember from the preaching was the preacher telling everyone they were good and God loved them. Those preachers never told us the whole truth."

The State School (CDC) is no longer open. The campus remains a state institution but the buildings have been torn down. The campus now houses the more violent and mentally disturbed. Whether or not another Bill Reid lives among them or the conditions of the past have been fully corrected is unknown by this writer or by Bill and known only by those who are there now.

The campus in 2012 is patrolled by security. No one can enter the property without authorization. Bill visited the campus once or twice after his release but was promptly escorted off the grounds by security.

Sandy's Story: The School

THE county nurse told Earl and Esther there was a school in Columbus, Ohio that would take care of Billy. The school was located on the West side of Columbus within sight today of Interstate Highway 70. In the Spring of 1956 Esther and her married daughter, Betty, drove to Columbus with Billy and turned him over to the supervisor at CDC.

The rambling red brick buildings were packed with residents at the height of its use. Sandra Jackson worked at State School as it was called from May 1969 until April 1972. Sandy remembered the buildings packed with clients, both adults and children. In her opinion many of them did not need to be there, they simply looked different or walked differently from what their parents or caregivers considered normal but there was no alternative for them in Ohio at the time.

Years after her employment at State School ended Sandy became acquainted with Bill Reid. They attended the same church in Columbus. Sandy was amazed at Bill's accomplishments after his release from State School. Since her tenure was after Bill's confinement she knew nothing of the troubled childhood and adolescent abuse he suffered but she witnessed first-hand the treatment of residents during her employment. It was hard for her to picture this gentle, kind, caring, and out-going man as a former resident of the school. The impact Bill made on people in the community and church as a mature adult was incredible.

Sandy moved to Columbus in her early twenties. An advertisement placed in the Columbus Dispatch offering employment at the state run school caught her attention. She circled the ad and wrote above it, "My Job!" She called for an interview and landed the job.

Sandy had no idea the kind of school CDC was. The staff took her on a tour of the area she would be working in after she accepted the position. She was shocked by what she saw. There were naked children sitting on wooden benches with soft restraints around their arms. Some were restrained both by their arms and legs. Some of the children were sitting in their own feces and urine. The smell was overpowering. She left the school that day thinking, "I can't do this." She called her mother crying. "I can't work at that place." Her mother encouraged her to try it for three weeks and see if she felt the same way. Sandy was unemployed and any work was a welcome relief. Sandy accepted the position. Sandy referred to the occupants of the school as "clients." Her description of them serves as a graphic reminder of the ordeal Billy Reid faced as a thirteen-year-old abandoned by his parents and family. The clients Sandy worked with were considered profoundly and severely "retarded" but they understood a touch, a hug, or a kiss on the cheek. Sandy fell in love with her clients and determined to make a difference in them, even if it were little. She soon discovered that many of the residents were not "retarded" at all. They simply looked or walked differently from others. Because of their rejection by others many of them had behavioral problems but nothing deserving of the conditions they were kept in.

Her goals were to teach the children to dress and undress themselves, to eat with utensils, not to stuff food into their mouths with their hands. The children remained in one large room during the daytime. Around the wall were adult size "potty chairs" which Sandy used to "potty train" some of her clients . She also worked to teach them not to steal food. Unable to feed themselves properly or not knowing how to feed themselves may have accounted for their hungry attempts to "steal" food.

Sandy worked the two-o'clock to ten-thirty shift. After the evening meal the children were moved to a dormitory with row after row of cots where they were put to bed each night about eight o'clock. There were between thirty and forty beds in the room. The bathroom was a large room where residents were showered and toilet trained. When she left in April 1972 her clients were going to the dining room to eat their meals and keeping their clothing on most of the time. The skills she taught them were not learned overnight but she felt a sense of accomplishment from her days there.

Working at State School wasn't always pleasant. Sandy recalled being kicked, slobbered on and often punched by clients. There was no privacy for the residents. They had families somewhere but few had families who came to visit them or call them or check on them. The calls never came so the staff became their family.

Some of the clients like Billy Reid had behavioral problems. Many of their problems were related to their physical appearances. Their appearance and behavior made them socially unacceptable in their families and communities. Their parents and care givers did not know how to handle them so they placed them in CDC. The staff looked professional. Everyone wore white uniforms, white hose and white shoes. On the outside, CDC, was referred to as a school for the retarded. For the clients on the inside, it was a horrible place and a prison.

Sandy recalled that most of the staff she worked with treated the clients well and cared for them. However, there were a few staff members who mistreated clients. One male client was found with what appeared to be the bottom of a tennis shoe imprint on his back. The staff was questioned but no further investigation took place. Clients were segregated by gender and most of Sandy's work was with male residents ranging in age from seven to seventeen years of age. She was satisfied with her working conditions until she became pregnant in April 1972 and feared being kicked or hit injuring her unborn child. She left State School and never returned to work there. When she returned to work, she became an employee of the State School for the Blind.

Sandy's work experience supports the description of State School given by Bill after his release and the profound changes that took place in his life outside the school.

A Typical Day

D AYS in the "school" started at six in the morning. Residents were required to shower, four or five at a time. Breakfast was served at seven o'clock in groups. Resident dormitories were located near the mess hall and classrooms. At eight o'clock the residents of a group were sent to a "classroom" where they watched television all morning. The older, stronger kids were instructed to make the younger ones behave. The attendants would leave the room and the bigger kids would take over. Beatings were common. When the attendant returned no one dared tell what had happened.

Some of the kids in these groups were there for murder. Bill recalled, "I remember one resident whose offense was the rape of a two year old child on the outside. Some of the residents were not normal. Once a resident 'went crazy' and threw me out of my bed to the floor. I had no warning. He had no reason to attack me. It took four other kids to get him off me. The attendant came in and called for more staff. They gave the kid a shot to knock him out."

"One of the few privileges we had included a money credit card. Families sometimes sent money which was turned into the administration and issued as money credit cards. My parents gave me a small amount of money, usually no more than five dollars, which I used to buy candy to bribe the bigger kids. Kids were allowed to smoke with a parent's permission and the availability of money."

"I learned pretty quickly that the purpose of being in State School was to teach me to 'behave.' Behaving meant listening to instruction and doing what I was told to do. This included cleaning floors, restrooms, and dormitories. Some of the residents could not feed or clothe themselves properly, so those of us who could, learned to help them with their personal needs which earned approval from our instructors."

"We were allowed to go outside for one hour a day and then only in certain areas. An attendant would stay to watch us. Outside we were watched closely. There was a fence around the place but if we got caught outside the assigned area we were in big trouble. We got away with a lot but we knew not to get caught. If we got caught in the wrong area we were written up on a green sheet and our outside privilege taken away. We would have to clean the buildings or stay in our rooms for a period of a week or two or longer. The punishment depended on what you did and where you went."

"All I could think about each day was how to get out of there. We talked constantly with each other how we would break out, where we would go, and how no one would ever tell us what to do again. If I ever got out of there I would do what I wanted and no one would tell me what to do. A few tried running away."

"If you talked back to an attendant you were written up or placed in a small room. Sometimes an attendant would smack you if you talked back. The attendants had control. We were told they were able to add time to our stay at State School. At least, that's what they told us. Some kids never got out because they couldn't obey orders. The attendants told me that my family didn't want me. I felt it was true and that I might never get out. Attendants didn't socialize with us. Thinking about them now, I would call them anti-social types. Some of them were afraid of the older kids. They knew the things these kids had done to be placed there. They also threatened to tell what they knew about us. 'I know your record. I can tell others what you did to people outside.' "

"Some were in there for rape. Some were in there for murder. Some were just crazy. Some were in there because no one wanted them. There were dangerous kids living among us. When the violent kids got out of control, attendants would bring three or four men to restrain them and give them a shot to knock them out. When they came to they would be transferred to an area where they couldn't hurt anyone".

"Once, I was almost choked to death. This big kid went berserk and grabbed me by the throat. He was bigger than me and I couldn't fight him off. Four other guys got him off me. If they hadn't stopped him, he would have killed me. He didn't care what happened to himself. I was sitting on my bed when he grabbed me around my throat. By the time the others could get him off me, I had nearly passed out. He should not have been among us."

"Fear was a big factor in the school. No one dared tell anything to a parent or administrator. Somehow complainers were identified and more beatings and attacks came from the bigger kids. I saw kids fight to hurt one another. If we told anyone, we could get in more trouble. A thirty-year old or older went crazy. He picked me up and threw me across the room. Attendants had to restrain him, knock him out and transfer him away to Apple Creek, a place for the more uncontrollable."

"If anyone made too much trouble about what happened to them, the attendants would walk out of the room for five minutes and let the kids take care of the problem. Some of those kids ran that place. The women attendants were afraid of them and some of the male attendants, too. When I got out of there I did my own thing. It took me a long time to make friends or trust people. I didn't trust anyone."

"Once I started to listen to instruction the next step was assignment to a step-up group where trades were taught.

It took me three years to move into a trades group. I was about sixteen years old by this time. Life got easier. I was moved to another dormitory. There were fewer beatings. The rapes continued but were less frequent. I think the really bad ones were left with the incoming and weaker residents."

Christmas

66 **M**Y childhood memories of Christmas would not be considered normal by most families but since I didn't know anything else I loved Christmas. All the family got together on Christmas eve to decorate a Christmas tree. My brother, Donald, and I would walk into the woods surrounding our farm and find a tree, usually on someone else's property, cut it down and drag it home. Normally, Dad would get stoned on Christmas Eve. He worked all the time which was probably needed to support such a large family. Several of us kids drank a lot. I was drinking whiskey and beer by the time I was seven and eight years of age because it was always there."

"I interpreted our family life as freedom. We were allowed to do pretty much what we wanted. What we were not supposed to do, we knew how to slip away and do anyway. Me and my brother, Donald, and a younger sister would hide under the big table with a bottle of beer, wine or whiskey and see who could drink the most. We would drink until we got sleepy or passed out."

"Mother made wine for the family. She and Dad both drank as well as the kids. Mother never drank like Dad. My Dad would get pretty loaded and pass out and we would take the keys away from him to keep him from driving to work. Over the years he had several accidents while drinking. A big part of Christmas for several of us was about drinking and getting drunk."

"There were some normal activities along with Christmas. Mother would make candy. Our neighbors would come over and we would celebrate and return to their houses to decorate their trees. We would do stupid things. The kids would have snowball fights and run down to the neighbor's houses and do crazy things. Overall, we had good times at Christmas."

"Mother and Dad would make gifts for us. Most of our presents were clothes. We didn't get a lot of toys unless it was tinker toys or some small item like that. We had a big family and extravagant gifts and toys were not part of our Christmases."

"Christmas was fairly peaceful for the family even with all the drinking. The big ones didn't pay attention to the little ones. We would ride sleds and stay outside the whole day. We always enjoyed ourselves during the holidays. Nothing spiritual was brought up. We never talked about God or anything like that. We ate a lot. On Christmas Eve we went to bed early, at least we were sent upstairs to our bedrooms. My brother, Donald and I, would open the heat register that allowed warm air to drift upstairs to heat the room and watch downstairs to see what we were going to get. Our parents would be wrapping our gifts and we could see what each of us would get. One of those times I got caught in the open register and cut my head. Christmas morning we already knew what we were going to get. We had counted the gifts to see who got the most."

"I enjoyed the drinking. Being that small you would think we couldn't get alcohol but Mother made wine and hid it. We would find it and take it to our room and drink. We smoked. We would steal cigarettes from our older brothers and neighbors. Discussions that started between me and Donald seemed to turn into fights. I didn't like Donald and he didn't like me."

In later years Donald could not remember having a dislike for his younger brother which seemed strange given the bitterness that Billy felt in himself for Donald and the family. "When the fights started Mother would scream for us to stop. When we kept fighting, she came after us with a leather strap kept for the occasion. She would give our legs a solid whipping but it never seemed to stop the fighting. I really gave my mother a rough way to go. I was afraid of my Dad and didn't cross him but Mother was mad at me most of the time. She would shout, 'I don't know what I m going to do with you.' Left alone, Donald and I would go out an upstairs window and do something else."

"I remember singing Christmas songs during those times. Occasionally the kids would try to help around the house, too. But, most of the time we spent getting into some trouble. My problem was my unwillingness to listen. I would not listen to anyone older than I. My mind wasn't focused. If I had learned to listen I would have done better, I'm sure." Later, Bill reflected upon this lack of self-control and purpose as an absence of God in his life. "Without the Lord to control me I had no control. I was very fortunate to find Christ and invite him into my life. God restored control and meaning to my life. I don't know how anyone can make it through life without Christ. It's all that saved me."

"At State School in Columbus small groups would come each Christmas to sing carols for us. They would give us pipes and cigarettes. I got a pipe and tobacco for a Christmas gift when I was fourteen. When people came in to sing to us and wish us a merry Christmas I had a deep lonesome feeling and wished I could go home. Mother would call the school and tell them she couldn't come and get me. I became very bitter. I never said anything at school about my feelings. I kept everything inside of me and when I did go home I got into worse trouble because that anger was inside of me. I didn't know why I had to go back to State School when I came home."

"The truth was that they couldn't put up with me. I was always looking for trouble. At school I got into fights and some trouble, too. I was very lonely. I didn't trust any of the other kids or any of the staff. That feeling of isolation and loneliness stayed for years after I left State School. As I got older and got free to do my own thing, there was always that empty feeling. My brothers back home had girl friends or wives but I didn't have anyone. It made me feel I wasn't good enough or capable of having a relationship with anyone. I didn't know how to talk to women. Even when I went out a few times with girls in later years I didn't know how to talk with one and have a relationship until I was much older."

"Christmas at State School was very lonely. I knew I was stuck there. I could watch television but whoever was the biggest got to watch what they wanted. I had to go to bed at a certain time. No one got close to me. The staff drew a paycheck. They went home at the end of the day. They didn't want to talk to any of the kids and get involved in what was going on in our lives. It wasn't a happy place or a happy time. No one ever talked to you about God except one attendant lady who only talked about the Revelation and hell. The food was not the best in the world. The Christmas singers would bring candy at Christmas or an apple or orange but they didn't talk to us. They just handed us a gift and we would go into a corner and trade with someone else for something we wanted. I remember once that I got socks. It was a very odd time. There were others who couldn't go home. Some didn't have families or they had violent records. The angry ones took it out on the younger. That's how I remember Christmas until my life changed."

A Ray of Hope

66 **I** GOT tired of being beaten up and started to listen to my instructors. They would teach us how to fix shoes. They taught trades in cleaning, cooking, making shoes and crafts. I made a few things. I started to listen. They told me if I didn't get it right, I wouldn't get out of there."

"I hated that place but it helped me. It helped me get my mind together. I went to school on the premises. I went but I had a mental block. I never could learn anything. I didn't understand."

"In spite of the awful things that happened in the place, I can see now how God used what happened to change me. By the time I was sixteen I started to learn a little. I learned to write my name. I remember my teacher, Mrs. Corey. She helped me learn to write a few words and write numbers. I still wanted out and I still had to deal with beatings but I was learning. I had never done that before."

"The school had a program that allowed those who showed signs of rehabilitation to go into the city for short day visits.

C. Nolan Phillips

Those in that program were considered employable and allowed to work jobs and return to the institution. All I could think of was how to get out of that place! Ungodly things were done to me. It happened to a lot of kids and nothing was ever done about it. After a trial period those who handled the outside work program well were sent to a halfway house to live until final release would be granted. I lived for the day I would be free. One day I intended to make it to a halfway house and after that to be free---on my own!"

"After I was released and after the miracle that changed me, I determined one day to tell my story so others could see the miracle that changed my life forever."

Billy's Story

"SOMEONE told me when I was still in grade-school that I was born for trouble. I believed them. At eight years of age, I started to drink. My brother, Donald, and I would drink all the beer we wanted. My mother made wine and we drank it. Growing up, our parents were pretty permissive and my younger brother and I did just about anything and everything we could. I suppose with all the kids and the problems my older brother, John, went through with his accident they were just too busy to manage each of us."

"Most of my memories of grade school were about fights. Kids would say things about my disabilities and call me names. I would fight them. Even though I was smaller than kids my age and had some physical disabilities affecting my speech and my ability to walk or run, my reaction to their taunts was to fight and hurt them if I could. I was pretty effective and by age nine the school teachers and administrators refused to allow me in school. They said that I couldn't learn because I wouldn't listen."

"Growing up with my younger brother, Don, I remember playing together. Sometimes we hurt each other. Don was two years younger than me but physically stronger. He was more coordinated and that made me more angry at him and jealous. Sometimes, I would hurt him worse than he hurt me. My parents would have to break up the fights. He and my younger sister would tease me because I couldn't climb a tree or drive a lawn tractor."

"I remember playing with them in an upstairs room when I decided to take an iron bed rail and kill them. My mother happened to come up the stairs as I raised the rail and she screamed at me, 'Billy, what are you doing?' I dropped the bed rail and ran downstairs and hid."

"By that time, both my mother and father had reached the end of their wits about how to handle me. They talked to a county nurse who went to the church my mother sometimes attended. They told her, 'We can't handle Billy anymore. We don't know what to do with him. We have to do something.' The nurse suggested they send me to the Columbus State School in Columbus, Ohio."

"They left me there and I hated them for it. Once a year someone from my family would come down and visit me. The school allowed me to go home one week a year to visit my family but they always told me, 'You have to come back to the state school.'"

"At State School my fighting continued. There were plenty of older kids and when I turned on one of them, I got beat up pretty badly. Some of these kids were eighteen and nineteen years old. I was only thirteen or fourteen. At least I wasn't one of the six or seven year old kids in the same room with us. The older boys did unmentionable things to them and sometimes to me, as well."

"You could say the older kids ran the 'classrooms.' When the attendants left the room, the older ones would take any kid who bad-mouthed them into the restroom and beat the daylights out of him. Plenty of times, that happened to me."

"I thought about running away but I didn't know where to run. Columbus was a big city. It was new to me. I hated the place. I hated my life. I hated my family but I had no place to run. I knew one thing, though. I had to get out of that place. I would find a way to get out."

"After a while I got tired of fighting back and just learned to go into a shell and that's how I existed. I was shy and backwards. I had a fear in my mind especially where I slept at night. I was afraid something would happen to me."

"I had no use for my family. I was cut off from them. So, I was on my own. I met some kids as I grew older. I was at Pine Ridge cottage on campus for three or four years. I went to Lincoln Village from there and things got better. My desire was to get out of the place as far away as I could. I had no use for it."

"State School made me think about a lot of things. I decided to find out how to get out of there. Once a month we were allowed to talk to a social worker or a psychiatrist. They would put me through tests. I had to draw. I would look at the pictures and they just looked like bombs going off. I learned that was the wrong thing to say. I remember my social worker telling me that the pictures were about butterflies. So, I would tell them the pictures made me think of butterflies. If that's what you needed to say so they would let you out, I'd sure say it. But, they did look like bombs going off to me!"

"Kids about my age and a year or two older were allowed to hang out together but we couldn't see any of the girls. I wasn't interested in girls anyway. Occasionally there was a get together and we could talk to them. I didn't have a girlfriend. I stayed away from anybody acting like me. I stayed away. I must have done something terrible to get there. I didn't learn a lot there. I didn't even know how to spell my name. A Mrs. Cory tried to teach me a little bit. I didn't know how to read."

"Kids there would make fun of me and call me names. I remember that they called me 'Penguin Toe'. I didn't know anything was wrong with me till I got there and the kids told me. My family always treated me as being normal and I found out that I wasn't exactly normal or smart. Ron was one of my friends there. We always talked about getting out and living together on the outside."

"I thought if I ever got out of there I would never come back. I would rather be dead than there. One social worker told me I needed to listen to those in authority over me. I had to learn to listen and learn right from wrong. It helped. They began to trust me. They allowed me to take records to cottages or get ice for the kitchen from the ice house. She would give us chunks of ice for doing it."

"I worked in a shoe repair area and learned to polish and repair shoes. I learned to wash dishes and pots and pans. It kept me out of the place where I lived some of the time. The attendants were in charge there. They liked me because I would scrub floors, wash windows, set up tables…anything to please them."

"It was amazing to me to see people with no legs or arms; people who couldn't talk. They acted like babies but they were forty years old. This was a shock to my mind. We would have to change their clothes and wash them and feed them. We never were paid for it. I had a weak stomach and didn't want to do it but I had to. They told me I had to have a good record to get out. That scared me. I would do anything to get out of that place."

"One of the attendants working there, a woman, asked me once, 'Billy, if you die where would you go? Do you believe in hell? Do you believe in heaven?' I said, 'I'm not sure.'"

"A man who worked there asked me the same question. 'Do you believe in hell? Do you believe in heaven?' Then he told me, 'Everybody who dies goes to heaven. There's no such place as hell.' I liked that explanation. I could do anything I wanted and didn't have to worry about going to hell. So, that's what I believed during my teenage years."

"One of the supervisors over me was named Mrs. Brewer. This lady was very strict. I mean she didn't put up with anything. In some ways she was so strict she was mean. If she wanted you to do something and you didn't do it, she would smack you down and you would do it. It may not have been the way she should have treated us but it sure taught me to respect authority. She also had a kind side, too. She would tell you your faults. She tried to help us understand things. She would explain things on the outside of the school. Some state workers in the school would lie to you about the outside. They would tell you that once you got out of there, you would never have any more problems. You would be free to do this and that. Mrs. Brewer would tell you the truth. She didn't want you to be let down when you got out there in the real world outside. In some ways, I can look back and see how this lady really helped me, even if her ways were mean at times."

"I learned that Christians were different, some of them. There was one Christian lady who would tell me about God and the Bible and the book of Revelation and Hell. She never talked to me about Jesus or salvation. She never told me how to be saved. I never understood about salvation or Jesus. She never mentioned this. She would tell me I would burn in hell if I didn't do good things. I don't know what her reasoning was now that I think of it. She meant well but she didn't know how to present the Gospel and the love of God. I think she was a Pentecostal believer."

"I found a social worker on the staff and asked him, 'How do you get out of a place like this?' He said, 'Billy, you have to learn a trade and you have to learn to listen to instructions.' Listening was hard for me. I had never listened to anybody, but I had to learn to listen."

"Another worker there told me, 'Billy, you will never leave this place. You'll be here for good. There are others here older than you and some of them lived here until they died.'"

"I started listening to the staff who wanted to train me. I made friends with a few of the older kids and began to learn a trade. I washed dishes. I was determined to do anything to get out of that place. After a while, the staff noticed what I was doing and told me that if I continued behaving and working there was a chance I could get out."

State School Friends

"EVERYONE was on his own in State School. I had two or three close friends who had been sent there by their families and judges. One of them, Ron Phillips, looked out for me. Ron didn't have the physical handicaps I had. I'm not sure if his problem was mental or emotional. I do know that he had a hair-trigger temper and he wouldn't listen to anyone."

"Ron was a year older than me, about fifteen, when we first met. We were about the same height and weight which put us at a disadvantage with the older, tougher kids. We got along pretty well. In the five or six years I knew Ron, we only had one fight…over some girl on the street. Ron was a real down to earth kind of guy. Both of us saw pretty quickly that we needed each other to protect us from the bigger kids. These boys didn't play games! We needed somebody to look out for each other."

"We made friends with as many of the tougher kids as we could. They put the word out that we weren't to be messed with. It helped some. We found other kids like ourselves and formed sort of a protection group. If I wouldn't tell when someone beat me up, the others would let the word out. The tough kids learned not to mess with us or they would get grief from the staff."

"Ron was in Pine Ridge Dormitory when I arrived at State School. It wasn't as bad as the one I was assigned at first. I stayed in that first dorm for about eighteen months before being moved to Pine Ridge. We hit it off right away. I had to watch out for the black kids. Some of them were big, strong and tough. My first beating from one of the kids was from a big black kid who wanted to see how tough I was. After Ron and I got together, the word got around that we may be smaller but when you took on one of us, you took on both. It helped."

"Ron never told me why he was in State School. I sort of guessed that it was his temper. His family couldn't control him. He had an awful temper. He wouldn't listen to anyone. I was like that, too. If someone pushed me, they were going to get pushed back, even if it meant a beating."

"We volunteered to work in the school cafeteria sweeping, mopping and cleaning. All we talked about was 'When we get out of State School!' We weren't paid for the work but the attendants saw to it that we got some freedom around school."

"I remember Ron's family came to see him once in the years he was there with me. My folks came once a year most years to visit me at school. I was given a week at home on Christmas but always told, 'You have to go back to State School.' None of us dared tell what really happened to us there. Somehow word would get back and the big kids would come after us. Some kids never had a visit from anyone. They were there for life. They had been told like the rest of us that we were a danger to ourselves, to others and to our families."

"Ron and I earned the privilege of going into the city to halfway houses about the same time. We worked in restaurants and bars together. We stayed in the same halfway house. I didn't like the lady who ran the halfway house. She was paid by the state to give us a room and each of us had to pay her eight dollars a week to stay there. She wanted us to call her 'Mom' which I didn't like."

"Working in the bars and restaurants gave Ron and me the opportunity to sneak alcohol. We would take empty bottles and drain the contents to get drunk. The landlady didn't like our drinking so we had to be sure we didn't get too drunk to get back into our rooms without any trouble. If we had trouble, it was back to State School....for good! We were careful. We did some stealing, but we watched our step pretty carefully."

"In time, Ron got a job at Ohio State University in the kitchen. We met a few more times to drink and run around town. We always picked a place away from State School or where we worked to make trouble. We didn't want anyone recognizing us and sending us back. The last time I heard from Ron he had gotten married and sometime later I learned he had two kids. I'll never forget Ron. Our friendship made life bearable in State School."

"Another kid, Pat Burleson, hung out with us at State School. Pat was a big, tall kid. He was at least six feet, two inches in height but he was different from us. He did scary stuff. I did hear that he was put there because he raped a little girl about eight years of age. Pat was about three years older than I was but he hung out with me, Ron and a few others. He did stuff we wouldn't do. He constantly tried to pick up girls on the street. The age didn't matter. He went to halfway house with us. We didn't like to hang out with him because he would go into bars and roll drunks. He befriended them inside the bars and got them on the street where he robbed them of their money."

"Sometime in his early twenties, Pat went home to live with his family. I don't know what happened to him after that. He was dangerous because he would rob you. We were afraid of him and kept our distance from him. He was lucky not to be sent back to stay at State School permanently."

NEXT STEP

IN 1966, after eight long years of abuse and loneliness, Bill Reid, found a way out of Columbus State School. Looking back he realized the school had actually taught him basic survival skills in the outside world. When he finally processed that he was on the way to gaining his freedom, he started to listen to instructions and cooperate with the staff whenever he was given an assignment.

"After six years of my life in State School I started to beg the staff. I would go the office after I got old enough to go outside and look for a job. I would beg them to let me out. They would tell me, 'It's not time for you to go outside. You'll have to wait.' A year would go by and another year would pass and I really pestered the staff because I wanted out of that place. I had been told by staff over the years that I would never leave there. I would be there for good."

Billy's initiative to help younger, weaker residents feed and clothe themselves paid off. One day a social worker called Bill into his office and told him he was going to be placed on a trial release at a halfway house in Columbus. If he was able to find gainful employment and follow the rules of the halfway staff, it was possible that Bill could gain his release from CDC and be on his own. The rules were simple. Residents had to pay rent and find a job. Bill agreed to both terms. After six months of successful work Bill was given his freedom. He was told that he could find his own apartment and continue to support himself."

"By the time I was eighteen I had earned the opportunity to work at Goodwill Industries in Columbus. I was placed in the shoe division where I shined shoes, repaired soles and heels and made fifty cents an hour. Most of the workers in this facility were severely handicapped and I knew I didn't belong there. I was capable of more responsibility. I hated that place because I knew I was capable of doing better."

"As part of my work, training classes were offered to teach residents to read and write. I simply couldn't learn. I had an undiagnosed learning disability. Each day I would leave frustrated because I couldn't learn to read and write."

"I could learn city bus schedules and directions, but I couldn't understand words and letters. They assigned me to a room in the half-way house in Columbus where I stayed outside the state school for the first time. It was one step toward freedom but I had a long way to go."

"When I turned twenty years of age a state social worker interviewed me on a weekly basis. I convinced her that I could get a job in a restaurant. The worker agreed and I applied at a restaurant in Columbus for the clean-up crew at night. The next two years I lived in several half-way houses and worked restaurant jobs. I became 'the best pot and pan scrubber' in Columbus. I was on my way out of CDC....but not out of trouble."

During his confinement at State School male residents were not allowed to date female residents. Their dormitories and classrooms were separate from the boy's campus. Outside the school Bill had difficulty talking to girls he met. During his three-year work-release program Bill made no permanent friends. At the end of the three years the school signed a permanent release form and Bill was on his own.

Release from Half-Way

66 I FINALLY got my big break. I got a job on the outside at Goodwill industries. I earned $17 a week for work. I wasn't allowed to stay out at night. I saved a hundred dollars in the bank and the staff considered me a safe risk to be sent to a half-way house with eight other guys. I hated that place, too. The lady in charge would tell me what to do and I hated being told what to do. She was very strict. I was to stay there for three years on probation. I couldn't wait for that probation to end and be released on my own from the school. I knew what I would do. Nobody would tell me anymore what to do."

"Ron and I were assigned the same half-way house. We both needed jobs. I started at Goodwill Industries and then at a restaurant. I had to give the landlord eight dollars a week. I made thirty-five dollars every two weeks. I could do what I wanted with the rest. We would run around. We would go to Ohio University. My friend, Ron, had found a better job there. We had to be careful not to let people know where we were from but they found out somehow. If you were from the institution you must have done something bad to get there. They would watch you. "My landlady would call them up and say, 'He's from the state school.' The girls would hear that and take off. I thought something was wrong with me, too."

"When I was 21 years old I was old enough to get into a bar. That was the year I was released from the school. I went to the bar before I went to work and after I got off. When I went to work I drank. We would get bottles and when the boss wasn't there we would take whiskey, beer and wine bottles and drink. We would steal anything. I would walk into a store, put clothing on and walk out. I'm not proud of what I did. Before I became a Christian that's what I thought about. I stole clothes. I stole anything I got my hands on. People would trust me."

"My friends and I hung out doing things. One friend got married. One went home. Another died of a brain disease from drinking sterno. I was headed that way, too. I had other things on my mind. Some tried to talk to me. If I went with a girl it would break off because of the way I looked, walked and talked. All of this ate at my mind and my heart. I was very lonely. I was very gullible. I would try anything. It was the way I was. My friends went their way. I lost track of the people who were in the school with me. We would never tell anybody where we came from because they would distrust us. It would be harder to live. I wanted to get away from Columbus. I heard about California and wanted to go there."

"I went through a string of jobs. The main problem came when people working with me discovered I had been in State School. They thought I was either crazy or nuts or something. I wasn't crazy but people would still find out where I had been and I would lose my job. "

The day Bill was released from the state sponsored half-way program, he threw a party and drank himself drunk. He didn't have to answer to anyone. The taste of what he thought was freedom was definitely a first time high in his life. He could stay out all night. He didn't have to account to anyone.

His first job was at a local bar and restaurant where he cleaned the floors after the place closed at night. When he wasn't working, he was looking for trouble. Fights were common. Being as small as he was, fights usually went in favor of the other person.

Bill hated the world. His mother and father had sent him away to the school. They had tried to help him but Bill disowned them when he left CDC. He was on his own after that. He drank heavily. He took drugs. It was the sixties and the drug culture was in full swing. He did it all.

He worked at Olentangy Inn for five years on River Road. He started in the dish washing room and worked his way up to preparing salads. The cook and chef took up for him and helped him learn each job he was given. He had been a kitchen helper during his three-year probation and worked there for two more years before deciding to leave town.

Bill decided to leave Columbus. At work and in the neighborhood people soon found out he had been in State School and stories were told on him. The name-calling and jokes became unbearable reminders of his childhood and confinement.

Bill had saved some money. The half-way house had taught him the value of savings. The supervisor of the home gave each resident an allowance and banked the remainder. After five years Bill had a thousand dollars in the bank. Because of his association with the school and because people had bad opinions of those who had been there, Bill decided California would be better than Columbus, Ohio.

"I had been working with a buddy in a restaurant at nights. I had saved a thousand dollars. We decided to go to Los Angeles and see what life was like in L.A. Dumb me, I bought bus tickets for both of us and we spent four days riding across the country to California. I wasn't going back to Columbus again."

"The bus stopped at designated cities and then only for less than a half hour. I liked to talk to people and spent a lot of time talking to my friend and meeting new people. My buddy convinced me that L.A. was just the place to live. The temperature stayed in the seventies all year round. To somebody used to the winters of Ohio, I thought this must be like heaven. He also knew how to get us jobs where we could work."

"A young woman got on the bus somewhere along the way with a baby. Talking to her I learned that she didn't have any money left for food, not even milk for the baby. I thought of myself as a hard person from all that had happened in State School and back home but I couldn't let that baby go without milk, so I bought milk for the baby and some food for her. My buddy didn't eat much on the trip and I could tell he wasn't too happy that I was helping this girl. There was a reason."

"When we pulled into the Los Angeles bus terminal my friend told me we needed to go to a certain part of town on the city bus line. There were sleeping rooms available for seven dollars a night. I paid for a week and we moved in. There was a large open room where roomers could watch television. You put a quarter in the T.V. set and you could watch for an hour. My friend knew all of this. He had been here before."

"Everything went well for the first three days. My buddy and I went to the movies each evening. They showed four or five movies a night. We saw just about anything and everything. My buddy drank heavily while we watched movies. It only cost a quarter to get into the movies, much cheaper than paying for television back in the common room."

"My friend told me to watch out for the police. Little did I know but we were living on skid row in L.A. There were thousands and I mean thousands of homeless people living down there. They were sleeping in doors and on sidewalks and rescue missions. He also told me never to tell anybody I had any money, not even a dime. I saw people get beaten up on the street for a dime. He advised me to take the money I had which I had been carrying in my pocket, what was left of a thousand dollars and lock it in my suitcase in the room. The next morning when I woke up my suitcase and my Ohio buddy were gone. All I had in my pocket was twenty dollars. I had paid for the week or I wouldn't have had a place to sleep that night."

"My friend came back with another guy who threw me against a wall and put a knife to my throat. He knew I had twenty dollars in my pocket and he told me, 'Give me your money or I'm going to cut your throat.' And he would have done it, too! Then my buddy from Ohio told me, 'The reason I brought you to L.A. was to get that money you had saved.'"

Bill was scared---just like the early days in State school. Someone on the street told him about a place where they would give you something to eat and a place to stay. It was a rescue mission. It was a starting point. Without money he couldn't drink. He was twenty-five years old. He heard the story of Jesus in the mission but he didn't understand it.

"I didn't know what to do. I went down to the manager and told him how my money had been stolen. He told me, 'You should have put your money in the office safe.' He also told me

I was on my own as soon as the week's rent was up. Another renter heard about the mess I was in and I asked him, 'What can I do? Where can I eat?' He said, 'You can stay with me in my room.' He knew where we could eat at a rescue mission in the evenings. They served beans and cornbread, stuff like that. At least I had something to eat. But they preached to us while we were there. I didn't like that. I didn't believe in God."

"In the mornings I would go to another church where they gave me coffee and doughnuts....and preached some more to me. I hated it. I had to stay on guard for the police. They had big bakery bread trucks with lights on the top, painted dark green. They would patrol the streets and when they found you standing on a sidewalk, they would throw you in there and take you to jail. I learned how to get off the street and hide behind buildings so I wouldn't be arrested."

"One evening I didn't see the policeman until he caught me by the arm and asked me where I was from. I told him I was from Columbus, Ohio and my buddy had robbed me. He told me to keep moving. If he saw me standing still he would take me in. I grew hard on skid row. I didn't trust anybody. I didn't know how to get a job. I saw people getting beat up all around me. I begged for food."

"Someone sent me to a church where they preached to me and gave me food. I had heard about God from time to time growing up, but it never made sense to me. In State School, staff members would tell me stories about God and about Hell and it scared me. But, down on skid row without a friend on earth and nothing to eat I tried God out. 'God,' I prayed, 'If you help me out of the mess I'm in I'll go to church.' Next day I called my Mother and asked her to help me. She asked me to come home to Cleveland. I thought, 'They really do love me.' My Mother told me, 'The best thing for you to do, Billy, is go back down to Columbus.' I knew it…my family didn't want me. I went to a bar and started to drink."

"I stayed with anybody I met on the street. I did this for several weeks until my family sent me a bus ticket to Columbus. They didn't' trust me with money. They gave the bus driver ten dollars for me to eat until I got back to Columbus."

Return to Columbus

"WHEN I got off the bus in Columbus I went to the nearest bar and started drinking. Over the next several months I did everything to destroy my body because I cared less about living. I had no relationship with anyone. I was always in trouble. I started working again in a restaurant cleaning floors at night by myself. I was by myself. I was very shy. I had my own room. My landlady would leave me alone if I paid my rent."

"I found a job in a restaurant but my days were a haze of work, alcohol and drugs. I found a room with a family where I lived the next three years. I was now twenty-five years of age. The landlady took morphine for pain. She would give it to me occasionally to get high and I would steal it if she didn't give me enough. She got it legally and illegally. She finally had to be admitted to a rehabilitation center to kick her drug habit. I stole for alcohol and drugs and recognition. I drank more and more. I was going downhill physically, mentally and emotionally."

"The family I stayed with was very undesirable. The man stole things. I stole things for his family and they accepted them. I stole for their approval. They drank a lot and I drank with them. It was all I knew. I was always broke. These were really hard people. I couldn't break away from them."

"After I came back to Columbus, I could never earn enough or save enough money to be on my own. I had no real friends. My depression grew deeper and deeper. Finally, I decided to commit suicide. I saved enough drugs to end it all. Somewhere in my mind a voice began to say to me, 'What's going to happen to you after you die?' I couldn't shake that voice. I gave up on the suicide…for then. Looking back I realize that had someone offered me the hope and peace of God I would have gladly accepted the offer. When I finally discovered God loved me I realized that voice was His and He had warned me away from the danger I was in."

After Bill discovered freedom in Christ he was determined to find people who had given up on life or thrown on the scrap heap like himself. He boldly shared with them the peace he found. He was like one beggar telling other beggars where to find the bread. Now, at this low point in his life he heard God speaking but he didn't know who he was.

Before long the depression returned and this time Bill had a plan and enough alcohol and drugs to end his life.

The family he stayed with had lots of problems. "I met lots of street people in those days. One was the cook where I worked nights. He was killed by a train a few years after that. He would get drunk and fight. Any time I went with him I got into trouble and a fight. He had an idea how to get away from everybody and get out of the snow. He and another guy robbed somebody with a knife and got away. He was killed by a train somewhere. I could easily have been with him. There were times when I should have been killed by cars. On the street one night a guy threatened to cut my throat but I kept stealing and drinking."

"The hate I had in my heart for my family and people who picked on me was still there. It ate at me. I made a couple of friends among the workers. One of them in particular would go downstairs with me at the restaurant where they sent the beer, wine, and whiskey bottles. We would drink what was left in the bottles. We would drink as much as three bottles of beer and a couple of cups of whiskey a night. Someone told us we could strain sterno, which was 200% alcohol, through bread and we drank that stuff. It was real sweet and tasted pretty good. After my buddy went berserk drinking too much of it, I decided this wasn't for me and I quit drinking it. I even tried drinking shaving lotion for the alcohol; anything that had alcohol in it."

"To put it bluntly, I was deeply troubled. I was tired of living. I decided to do something to destroy myself. I had no friends, no family. I had become a thief as well as an alcoholic. I was at the end of my rope. I had had enough of life. I was going to commit suicide and get out. I would get even with my mother and father and family for what they had done to me. They'd be sorry."

"I collected a bunch of pills and picked a night to take them. I was working that night in the restaurant by myself. It was early in the morning and as I thought about suicide, a voice spoke to me again and said, 'What happens after you die? Is there a hell? Is there a heaven?' I looked around. I didn't see anybody. It scared me so badly I decided not to try suicide."

"Several times afterward, I met people who would bring up the subject of God and I would say to them, 'I don't believe in God. I don't believe in the Bible. I don't believe in nothing. Just leave me alone!'"

"Life ground on for me. At times, things got scary. One night a buddy and I were drinking. I was about twenty-six years old at the time. I was drinking pretty hard stuff; Vodka, I think. He said to me, 'I'm looking for a car to buy.' I said, 'Well, I can sell you a car.' I thought to myself, 'It doesn't belong to me but my landlord has a car he wants to sell. I'll sell him his car.' I told him to give me $350 and I would give him the car. I told him, 'You will have to hot wire it and you can have it for $350.' He agreed to the deal. He knew how to hot wire the car. We walked to my landlord's house after midnight. We opened the hood and he was working with the wires when I heard this loud voice yell, 'Halt or I'll shoot.' I looked up and my landlord was holding a shotgun out his window with it pointed at my head. I yelled, 'Don't shoot. It's me, Bill. Don't shoot.' The next day he told me, 'Bill, you don't know how close you came to dying.' God was watching over me after all."

Hitting Bottom

"I WAS so frustrated with life I didn't know where I was. One night I walked into the middle of a street without looking and suddenly realized a car was coming straight at me. I froze in my tracks. The car ran onto the sidewalk, hit a building, narrowly missing me. Again, God was watching over me but I didn't know it."

Bill's new prison was not made of chain fences, brick walls, and locked doors. He was a prisoner of his own mind. The walls he lived behind had been under construction for over twenty six years. He was filled with rage. His family was afraid of him. Billy thought getting out of CDC would make him happy. Instead, his life spiraled downward.

Suicide was continually on his mind. He had been working continuously. He had become tired of living. He was running drugs, drinking a lot, sick of his family and the world. A month after his last attempt at suicide was sidelined by the voice warning him, Bill's world seemed to be closing in on him. His job was going bad. Everything was going wrong. He had hit bottom. He didn't care if he went to hell or heaven. He was going to do it. This time he would get drunk and take pills and do it. He would end it all on Thursday night. Billy had hit bottom.

"That's when I determined to go through with suicide. This time I would get good and drunk. I wouldn't back out. It was a Monday. Friday was payday. That would be the day. I was looking forward to dying. I had nothing to live for. I didn't care if there was a hell. I was going to get out of life."

"On Tuesday evening a couple living across the street from me came over to my porch. They had lived there for more than a year. They invited me to go to their church. I said, 'No, I don't believe in God. Leave me alone!' I slammed the door in their faces. I went inside and upstairs to my room. My landlady listened to the couple and agreed to go with them on Wednesday. They all went to church that Wednesday."

"The following night, a Thursday, I came out of my room and started down the stairs. One more night of living and it would be over. My landlady saw me coming down the steps. She said, 'A preacher is coming over to see you tonight.' I said, 'I don't want to see any preacher!' She said, 'Well, all he will do is invite you to go to church.' I told her, 'I don't want to go!' She said, 'You don't have to go!' Just listen to him.'"

Free at Last

"I KNEW what I would tell that preacher when he came. That evening he knocked at the door. He didn't look much like a preacher to me. He was big, over 250 pounds. He wore glasses but he had no bible with him. I thought to myself, 'He couldn't be much of a preacher.' He sat down in the living room and asked my landlady, 'What's a Christian?' She said, 'A Christian is somebody who believes in God and goes to church.' The preacher said, 'Well, that's what Christians should do but that doesn't make you a Christian.'"

"He got up and sat down beside me. That made me nervous. He said, 'Bill, do you mind if I show you in the Bible what a true, born-again, Christian is?' I said, 'I don't know.' He said, 'Well, let me show you.' He quoted from the Bible, 'For all have sinned and come short of the glory of God.' When he said, 'All have sinned, every wrong thing I had ever done life flashed before my eyes!'"

"I didn't like what I heard. I wanted to get up and leave but I couldn't move. I couldn't do anything but sit there. He quoted again from the Bible. 'For the wages of sin is death but the gift of God is eternal life through Jesus Christ our Lord.' He explained to me that we deserve death but God has a gift of eternal life for us. Then he said, 'Billy, if you were the only person on the face of the earth, God would still send His son to die for you because he loves you.' That was the first time I could remember anybody ever telling me that they loved me. I didn't remember my mother, my father, my brothers or my sisters ever telling me that, even though I know they must have said it. When he told me that, my heart just broke inside of me. I didn't see any flashing light or hear any voice. I just got down on my hands and knees and asked God to forgive me of my sins. I asked God to come into my life and change my life and Christ came into my life and changed me."

"All the hate drained out of me. I know it's hard to believe after all the hate I had dumped on people. All the frustration emptied out of me. God changed my life at that moment. The preacher said, 'Bill, there's some things you need to do. You need to talk to God every day. You need to read your Bible and you need to go to church and you need to be baptized.' I bowed my head and thought, 'I can do everything I need to do but one thing. I can't read.' I was afraid to tell the preacher I couldn't' read. I didn't' know what to do. But, I knew I was different. "

"I went to work that night and told my boss. 'Something happened to me tonight. I accepted Christ.' He said, 'Bill, you're crazy!' I said, 'I might be crazy but I know what happened to me.' He said, 'Okay.'"

"I remember being on my hands and knees scrubbing the floor and the presence of the Lord just came into my heart. His power and His presence just surrounded me, His love and mercy filled my heart. I felt wonderful. I knew God loved me. I remember going home that night and going to my room. I said, 'God please help me to read your Word. I opened my Bible to Matthew 11:28 which says, 'Come unto me all you that labor and are heavy laden and I will give you rest.' Somehow I understood what it said. I'll never know how that happened. All I know is that I asked God to start showing me His Word so I could read it and share it with other people and He did.

Harold Smith, the pastor who introduced Bill to Christ told him that he could help others make the same decision by using the words of the Bible. He gave Bill some tabs and numbered each tab. Then he told Bill, "You start with the number one. Show a person the scripture and turn to tab number two. By the time they read all ten tabs they will either accept Christ or reject Him. All you have to do is say, 'Here, read these words.'"

Bill would go and find people and talk to them. He would tell them how God changed his life and tell them how much God loved them and then show them his Bible and ask them to read from it. Afterward, he would ask them, "Would you like to know Jesus? If God can change me, He can change anybody."

It was as if someone had turned on the light in a dark room. For the first time in his life Bill had a reason to live. He knew he was deeply loved by God. It changed his life. He couldn't wait to tell people about it.

God began to use Bill in a tremendous way. He would get up in the morning and ask God, "Use me today." He was encouraged by Pastor Smith who told him, "Bill, if you really want to know how God can use you, just ask Him. If God wants you to talk to someone about Jesus, He will show you a way."

Westside Baptist Church in Columbus was in the inner city of Columbus, only a few miles from the school where Bill had lived for the past eight years. The focus of the church was the down and out inner city people of Columbus. After his encounter with Christ the preacher told Bill, 'Why don't you call your mother and tell her what happened to you.' "I did. I called my Mom and told her what I had done. I told her, 'I don't understand this but God has saved me and I asked him to come into my life and He did.'"

Pastor Harold Smith told Bill he needed to do five things as a new Christian. He should go to church. He should tell others about Christ. He should pray. He should be baptized in obedience to Christ's command. And, he should read the Bible. Bill did the first four! But, he couldn't read. He was embarrassed to tell the pastor he couldn't read. He kept it to himself for a long time.

Bill knew that he had been given something. Jesus Christ became real to him. He was more real to Bill than people around him. Bill fell in love with Jesus Christ. He had no family or friends but now he had Jesus and knew he was deeply loved by Him. He asked God to teach him. He began to learn. He began to understand what was read to him. God taught him patience. "God gave me patience," Bill exclaimed. "You can't believe the patience He's given me."

Bill thought, "I can do all but read. I didn't want to tell the pastor that. I never went to school. They threw me out in third grade. The teacher told me I would never learn anything. I was beyond learning. All I wanted to do was fight. The only reason I fought was because people would pick on me. I would fight all the time; brothers, sisters, anyone. I got into trouble for it. I had a bad attitude about it. When the Lord changed me, He took away the hate and gave me love. He changed my life. He saved me."

"The Lord intervened time and time again to save me. The Preacher told me that night and God told me this was my last time. If I rejected Him this time it would be my last time. We think we have all the time in the world but we don't."

Bill recalled, "I remember being alone at work on my knees scrubbing the floor and the Lord just came in his power and glory and surrounded me with his love and mercy and I felt tremendous. I went home and upstairs I fell on my knees and said, 'God please show me how to read your word and the Lord showed me Matthew 11:28. It says, 'Come unto me all you that labor and are heavy laden and I will give you rest.' I asked God to show me His Word so I could read it and share it with other people. I wanted my story to show others how God can change our lives."

"I didn't know anything about God. When I was looking for God after I was saved I wanted to know more about Him. Pastor Smith showed me a promise in the Bible. It said, 'Come to me, all *you* who labor and are heavy laden, and I will give you rest.' Matthew 11:28 It was one of the first Bible verses I learned. I prayed, 'God, show me something that will help me.' I would put my finger in the Bible and turn to a page and find words to help me. The Bible is a living Word from God. I would listen to what God is saying. The promises seemed to jump off the page for me. Pastor Smith would tell me, 'Billy, all you have to do is ask God and He will show you what to do. Ask him to show you.' Another great promise taught me to listen and wait on God. 'Trust in the LORD with all your heart, and lean not on your own understanding...' (Proverbs 3:5) I told people I met that God will direct you and take your hand and put it in His Hand. Plenty of times I started down a road and took a branch off the right road. God would speak to me and tell me how to get back on the right road."

The unique difference in Bill Reid's story and that of other "thrown away lives" was the dramatic change that took place in him in a single moment without psychiatric or medical assistance. Knowing God was not a process but an instant change, a miracle of God. Bill was transformed from a God hater and a people hater to a God follower in a single moment. Twenty-eight years of rage was exchanged for a bold excitement for the One who changed him. Once again God revealed His delight in finding one the world has given up on and picking that person up and saying, "I can use you." Bill Reid was one of those.

Betty's Story

BETTY was fifteen years-old when Billy was born. She was endowed with the take-charge characteristic of the first-born. She was the only one allowed to hold or carry the tiny baby when Billy came home. Betty recalled Billy's birth vividly in later years.

She married in her teen years and had two children only two or three years younger than Billy. As Billy grew older and became more aggressive, she became increasingly fearful for the safety of her children. It was Betty who was given the assignment to accompany her mother on the hundred and twenty mile drive to Columbus one winter morning with thirteen-year old Billy leaving him in the care of the State School for the Handicapped, called CDC.

In her late seventies Betty still talked about the change in her younger brother, Billy, after his release from CDC. Her own children grew up and found rewarding careers. One of them, blinded early in life, became a computer chip designer. Betty proudly pointed out that he had done well financially.

Each of her three children turned out well. Responsibility for her three young children interfered with Betty taking her mother to see Billy in Columbus every year. Earl never visited Billy at all. The thirteen family members gathered on holidays and at Christmas. Someone would usually bring Billy up from Columbus. Betty recalled, "We were poor people. Our Grandfather on my Dad's side was a house builder. My Dad was a painter. I would watch him paint. My grandfather would build things. Dad later gave us ten acres to build a house on. We built a house in Hamden. Later, in 1986, we were able to sell it and build another house. Selling it, we built the last one and it is now free and clear."

"I was fifteen years old when Billy was born. I still remember how little he was. We carried him around on a silk pillow. Mother kept information about all the kids; how much we weighed at birth; our height, weight, and so on. She wrote down the days and the times each of us were born. Billy was born at 3:15 AM in Robinson Memorial Hospital in Ravenna."

"Eight of us were born in Geneva, Ohio. Homes in that era were not fully modern. We had running water but not hot water. In 1941, Dad moved us into the country outside Ravenna in Salyersville, Ohio. It was just a crossroad; no store or gas station. We were seven miles North of Ravenna on state route 44. That's where we were living when Billy was born. We only lived there six months after his birth."

"Dad had been a painter. He went into a factory in 1941 to make ammunition but, after Billy was born, and in the Fall of 1943 we moved to Chardon, Ohio where Dad worked in a chemical plant in Painesville, Ohio until he retired in the seventies. Dad drove trucks part of that time. "

"Mother fell into a cooking stove the morning before Billy's birth. (Esther remembered it as a porcelain covered kitchen table.) Her whole left side was black and blue. The hospital didn't do anything for Billy after his birth. They kept him warm with hot water bottles. They thought he would die. We kept him warm with water bottles when he came home. After Billy was brought home we had to listen to hear him cry. He hardly made a sound. His eyes and arms would tell you he was crying but there was no sound. I was the only one allowed to carry him. I loved dolls and I loved my little baby brother and sister. I would roller skate around the block and push him in a baby buggy. I helped by keeping Billy quiet and sleeping."

"When he was hungry he would cry. He would scream his head off and it would sound like a little peep. He didn't have the energy to do otherwise, I guess. It got louder as he grew older. He was a good baby."

"I remember many of the changes that happened in his life, like when he began to walk. He was about three and a half or four years old before he walked. Everything he did was late. Another baby boy was born in April 1945. Billy was born in March of 1943. Mother and Dad named him Donald. When

Billy was five the younger baby was walking and crawling, Billy became terribly jealous of Donald. Donald could do everything and anything. Donald was called Don but Billy was always called Billy and not Bill."

"Mom and Dad tried to be fair to Billy but he couldn't understand their unwillingness to let him do things Don did. Don and Ruth had blue ribbons for perfect health but Billy had none. Don had curly blond hair. Billy didn't. Billy didn't have any other health issues. He looked normal except for size. He should have gotten a blue ribbon for attending school or something. Why not? I have a picture of Billy sitting on the ground the day we took him to Columbus. He was sitting next to a suitcase. There he was, Mom and Billy and the suitcase, on our way to Columbus."

"In the late forties when Billy was seven or eight, Don could run and pick up things and the jealousy grew worse. Billy never went to school. They wouldn't take him. Mother tried but they said they couldn't teach him. He was so jealous of other kids and Don that he was unmanageable. He was thirteen when he was sent to the state school for the retarded. He went there in 1956."

"I had two boys by then. The first was born in 1948 and the second in 1951. Our little sister, Ruth, was born in December 1951. With Don's birth there were six boys. There were four girls. Ruth got lots of attention as the youngest and Don was allowed to do everything."

"Billy's jealousy became so noticeable that Mom and Dad worried that Billy would kill Don and my younger son, Lowell. He would look at you like he could kill you. Dad never disciplined Billy. He never beat any of the kids."

"I lived in Hamden, Ohio. My husband and I built our home there. Two more of my children were born then. Before I moved out, I would watch the kids and Mom could then go to the store. I worried that my kids born in 48 and 51 and Don in 45 could do anything and Billy couldn't. He looked at them with such hate in his eyes. A county nurse went to my church and she called on Mom because Billy didn't go to school. I would talk to her at church and she's the one who got Billy into the state school for the retarded. Mom and I took him down there."

"Billy was told that he was going to a school that would help him and he would live there. The family didn't know anything about the school except what the county nurse told us. It was in Columbus, Ohio. They had a school for the retarded. Billy didn't realize until we got there what was going to happen. Mom and I just took him down. The person in charge took him. Billy turned and looked at us like he could kill us. He thought we were throwing him away."

"They did teach him a lot there. They would take him into the outskirts of Columbus, give him a small amount of money, and he had to make it back to the school. When we saw Billy at the school he would be swearing like all the other boys. The minister who came to the school would correct him but Billy paid him no attention."

"We rarely went to see him. Money was tight. I had three kids. It was hard to visit. He wasn't allowed to come home. I think we did get him for Christmases. We had a brother who was crippled from a car wreck in 1938. His treatment over the years Billy lived at home had a lot to do with the amount of time and attention that could be devoted to Billy. We had a lot of family problems."

"At home Billy played with matches. I would go down to watch the kids while Mom went to the store on payday with Dad. Billy had to be watched. He was jealous of Don and Ruth. Once he burned down the chicken house in our back yard. It's any wonder one of those younger kids had not been in there when he did it. I wondered if he meant them to be in it."

"We hid all the knives. Billy would find a butcher knife and hide it under his bed. The county nurse was scared to death for the other kids that he would kill them. If you scolded him or said, 'Billy, bring that back here, he would look at you as if he would have thrown a knife had it been in his hand.'"

"Our entire family saw all of this. We were terrified what he might do. Mom was afraid to go to sleep at night for fear Billy would kill the younger kids. Billy was very strong in his arms. It was scary. I lived seven miles away. The other kids loved to visit me because they didn't have to fear Billy at my house."

"After the change in Bill and long after State School I could talk to him for the first time and get a decent response back. I was a Christian but my husband and my crippled brother would go to the bars. My husband didn't drink but went with a younger brother who did drink."

"Bill got in touch with us after his change to let us know what had taken place in him. He went to work at the Lifeway Book Store in Columbus handling all the mail orders for the store going all over the country. We were amazed. He handled that job like a normal person."

"We had a big house then. My brothers helped to build it. Later on when Billy married, he and his wife and children would come and visit us. In 1989 and 1990 my parents died nine days apart. Billy and Sheena would come and help on weekends. Billy met Sheena in Columbus. Billy was very helpful. They were a delight to have visit. It wasn't like the old days. What happened to Billy was just a miracle."

Don's Story

DONALD Reid was born in the hospital at Ravenna, Ohio just outside Charden. He was two years younger than Billy. Amazingly, his recollection of those childhood years held no recollection of hostility toward his older brother. In fact, his memories of his angry younger brother in later years were more pleasant than critical. Don was closest to Billy in birth.

Because of Billy's learning disabilities Donald and Billy were in grade one and two together. "Billy was held back in school because of his inability to learn and his size. He was much smaller than other children his age. However, his mind was more mature and he was constantly in trouble in the classroom. Since he couldn't read, he would take my homework and scribble his own name on it. By this time Billy had been examined by a child psychiatrist who recommended that the two of us be separated in school."

"On the playground Billy was my protector. He could really fight! At home we played cowboys and Indians just like normal brothers. When it snowed we sledded together. Those were good times with Billy. Once Billy stole a bicycle from a neighbor for me to ride. It was an old one but I learned to ride it. We would pass time turning pages through catalogs dreaming about toys we couldn't afford. I really wasn't aware of the anger issues Billy had or his jealousy toward me. My mother and older sister saw things a lot differently."

"After Billy was sent to Columbus, I remember his Christmas visits at home. We rarely visited Columbus. Things just went on at home without Billy. After Billy got out of State School and after things changed for him the two of us renewed our bond and have stayed close to each other."

Rescuing the Perishing

AFTER the miraculous change and spiritual growth in Bill's life he returned to live with his parents in Painesville, Ohio for several months. He was twenty-eight years old at the time. He had been very ill in Columbus and needed a place to stay. He soon recovered and began working in the Home Restaurant. His supervisor was a Christian woman. She told Bill he could talk to anyone who came into the restaurant about Jesus Christ if they would listen. He had all the freedom to talk to people about the Lord that he wanted. He thanked her repeatedly for the liberty and asked her, "Will you pray for me that God will use me to introduce people to Christ?" And, God did. He talked to police officers who stopped for coffee. He talked to kids who came in for a sandwich.

The restaurant was a stopping place for several young prostitutes. In his three years at Painesville some of these young women turned to Christ through Bill's conversations with them. As a result he was often threatened by those making money from their trade. It was one of the reasons Bill left Painesville three years later. The threats became too many and too frequent.

A gang of kids stopped regularly. One of them was a girl, a prostitute. Bill would talk to her. It was evident that she had been beaten at times. He would pour her coffee and tell her, "God loves you. No matter what you have done, God still loves you and wants to change you." He would tell the boys in the gang the same thing but they really weren't interested in anything to do with the Lord.

One afternoon while he was working, Bill saw the young girl with a swollen and bleeding face. She came to Bill and he said, "Why don't you go to the bathroom and wipe the blood off your face." She came out and he gave her a cup of coffee and she asked him a question. "Billy, would you go out with a girl like me?" Bill had made a choice never to go with a person who was not a Christian but he felt God wanted him to go with her. He made a date to go.

He asked her, "Where would you like to go?" She said, "I would like to go to a movie." There was a movie across the street near where Bill lived, so he agreed to take her. Then she said to him, "Billy, promise me that you will not touch me in any way; that's all I have, men just touching me, doing all kinds of stuff." Bill promised, "I promise you, I won't."

He took her to the movie which was a Walt Disney movie and they sat through part of it. There was a scene with animals running around. It seemed she was enjoying herself and she asked, "Is heaven like this?" Bill said, "Well, heaven's something like this, but this isn't heaven." She asked, "Well, could you tell me about heaven?" They left the movie and Bill took the girl to the pastor's home in Painesville. He wasn't present but one of his staff was.

Bill told him, "This girl wants to be saved." He said, "I'll take her into my study and we'll talk for a while. I want you to stay out here." Bill agreed. The pastor led the girl to accept Christ. About two hours later, she came out and hugged Bill and thanked him and said, "I'm changed. God forgave me for all my sins. God changed me." She said, "I'm calling my mother and father. They live in Cleveland, and I'm going to ask them to let me come home." Bill learned later that her parents were missionaries in Cleveland and the girl returned home to live with them.

After his evening with the girl, the boys in the gang were angry and upset with him and threatened to beat him up or kill him. They were losing big money from the girl's absence. Bill told them, "God will take care of me. You can't hurt me because I did what God told me to do." And then he told them, "God loves you, too."

Later, he met one of them on the street. He must have weighed 175 pounds or more. He asked Bill, "What would you do if I slapped you?" He said, "Well you can't do that because I have angels all around me." As soon as Bill said it, the kid looked at him in a strange manner and took off running down the street as fast as he could run. Bill never saw him again after that.

Bill kept reaching out to kids on the streets. He met seven teenage boys on the streets and talked to them about his encounter with God. Every time he met these seven boys, the Lord impressed him to talk to them and invite them to church.

One Saturday night he met them and they asked if he wanted to go for a ride with them. Bill responded, "No, I have to work." One of them said, "Okay, but, since tomorrow is Sunday, we'll all meet you at church. See you." Bill said, "You've been telling me this for years but you never show up." They chimed in, "Oh, yes we will."

They went for a ride that night down a country road. A dog ran in front of their car and they hit a tree killing five of them. The sixth lived but was in a coma for several months. Bill would visit him and pray for him and talk to his parents. He finally came out of the coma but Bill lost contact with him. He never learned if the boy turned to Christ or not. It made him realize just how quickly time runs out. Looking back at the meeting with the boys, he knew God was telling him to talk to them because their time was running out.

Fresh Start

BILL returned to Columbus after living three and a half years with his parents. He looked up one of his old employers and asked for a job in the kitchen. His old boss asked if he would be interested in being a cook. Bill had learned the basics of a chef in his previous restaurant work. Although he didn't know a great deal about the art, his biggest problem remained his inability to read. His prayer to God became, "I don't know what to do because I can't read." Restaurants have menus. They have cookbooks. Bill couldn't read the material assigned to the chef or the menu for the day.

Bill was employed as a cook at David's Buffet. It was much simpler than a restaurant. He was surrounded by people who knew what they were doing as cooks. He learned from them and God prompted him to listen, a skill he had concentrated on in CDC, and he learned the routine and skills needed.

He learned quickly. He became a Sous Chef! A Sous chef is the second in command in a kitchen. In French, the term literally means "under chef." Sous Chefs are an important part of the restaurants they work in, ensuring that everything runs smoothly whether or not the head chef is present. The duties of a Sous Chef vary widely, depending on the restaurant and its command structure. This position in the culinary world can be extremely demanding, especially since it carries none of the glamour associated with being a head or executive chef. Bill's duties often included ordering the food for the buffet from vendors.

Bill insisted that the Lord showed him how to do his job. He would ask one of the kitchen workers to go into the office with him and read off the menu for the day. Then, he called in the items needed. It was a plan that only God could have worked out and it worked perfectly for Bill.

The buffet had an assistant manager who had anger issues and spiced his conversation with curses. He treated the employees badly. Bill told him, "I have a policy when you come back in the kitchen that there will be no swearing back here. I won't allow it." The assistant manager tried it on several occasions and Bill promptly told him about the Lord!

His response was, "I don't care. I'm going to do what I want to do." "Not back here, you won't. You can do whatever you please in the dining room because you're over that area but back here, I'm boss." Bill retorted.

In that position Bill continued to influence and lead people to decisions of faith in Christ. He had some real challenges.

One of the workers told him, "I belong to the devil. I gave my heart and soul to the devil." Bill replied, "Well God can take that away." Then he discussed with the boy how the Lord would do this. The young man then said, "Tomorrow when I come to work, I'm gonna come in an hour early and I want you to tell me how to be saved. I have to go somewhere but I'll be back tomorrow." He never returned. Bill never heard from him again. He often wondered if the young man took to heart what he told him that day.

Some of those he talked to did return. A young man he met in the buffet met Bill ten years later and hugged him and said, "Thank you, Billy, for telling me about Jesus. I found the Lord about ten years after I left here." Bill thanked him and told him he was happy for him.

Some were like the assistant manager. They refused to listen and were unwilling to change. One day, Bill just got sick of hearing the curses and said to the Lord, "If I go to work and this man comes in and cusses at me or my help, I'm going to quit." He had no job, but he was determined to quit if he had to work in this kind of environment. Sure enough, the moment he got to work the assistant manager came in swearing at him. He was in an unusually foul mood.

Bill said to him, "I quit." He said, "Well, you can't do that." "Oh, yes, I can," he replied. So he quit the job with the assistant threatening him that he would never find employment in restaurant work again. He was right. Bill went to nearly every restaurant in Columbus asking for a job. He would tell them what he did and why he did it and they would not hire him. Their reason was, "You're not qualified to work here. You're not qualified to do what we do, so we can't hire you." Bill asked if he could be hired as a dishwasher or cleaner because he needed to work. Again, the decision was, "No."

It may have been his physical appearance; an obvious limp and voice impediment that made employers think he would fall and hurt himself bringing a big law suit. They refused to hire him.

At this point, Bill turned to his pastor, Harold Smith. "Do you know where I can find a job. I don't know what to do." He told Bill, "God will provide you a job, Bill. Just wait on the Lord. What you need now is to grow as a Christian. Our congregation is meeting in a large house and there's an extra room where you can live. You can pay the church $50 a month, when you find a job.

Amazing things happened during his unemployment. People would approach Bill on the street and hand him money and say, "Here's $10, $20, $30. All kinds of money would come to him. It was enough to pay his bills. He had enough to eat. But, he needed a job.

Baby Steps

ALTHOUGH there were dramatic changes in Bill's life, the road to emotional and spiritual maturity was marked with setbacks. Dramatic changes don't prevent moral lapses of judgment. Storms come, even for the followers of Christ. The changes in Bill's life were miraculous but he made plenty of mistakes. On the positive side, he joined Pastor Harold Smith's small Baptist congregation in the West side of Columbus. He found a family of faith who believed in him and understood the changes that had taken place in his life.

After his conversion Bill continued to meet new people. Within himself he discovered a strong interest in people and identified with hurting people. Shortly after returning from Painesville he met a woman in Westside Church to whom he was deeply attracted. Bill was still a lonely person. He had dreamed of having a normal life with a wife and kids. The young woman to whom he was attracted had been previously married. She had two small children. A friendship developed between them and they began to share the disappointments each had experienced. Bill fell head over heels in love with her and her children.

He knew this woman had been deeply hurt by the death of her husband and suffered from other relationships with men. She confided that she did not want to be married again. Bill was not convinced. For weeks he tried to find the courage to ask her to marry him. He expressed his fear to the pastor's wife who advised him to ask her personally how she felt. Instead, Bill made a cassette tape of his intentions and asked the pastor's wife to deliver it to the young woman. She didn't accept his offer of marriage. Bill was overcome with all the old feelings of rejection from the past. In spite of the changes he had experienced, he was devastated.

In the past when Bill encountered rejection, he determined to find some way around the obstacle. Another woman had recently begun attending the church Bill attended and he focused his hurt and attention on her. After a whirlwind courtship Bill married her over the warnings of several friends and the objection of his pastor. His new wife had been previously married and had seven children.

In his loneliness and newfound freedom Bill had not taken time to know the woman. Eventually she told him she didn't love him and only married him to use him to take care of her kids and there was nothing he could do about it. He was stuck in a bad marriage. He tried to work things out. He treated his step-children kindly. In his new faith in Christ he believed God would work everything out. Things got worse. His wife became involved with other men. Her former husband appeared on the scene and it looked as if someone was going to get hurt badly.

She was a good liar and stubborn about what she wanted. The marriage lasted less than a year. The experience cost Bill thousands of dollars he had earned and a large debt he had not earned. His step-children continued to contact Bill over the years following the divorce because he treated them kindly. But Bill's peace of mind and self esteem was badly damaged by the relationship. He had been taken in by a faithless wife.

He also learned not to run ahead of God no matter how strong your feelings. He learned to ask for wise counsel before entering into a relationship. He gained a new understanding of the suffering of an unwanted divorce. In it all he determined that divorce was not God's plan nor was marriage to a woman who was not also a follower of Christ.

Bill sincerely wanted his old acquaintances to know and experience this newfound joy he had. The problem was that these associates had neither the desire nor intention of changing their ways. For the next three years he tried to walk a narrow line between his new life and his old life. That led to several serious lapses of moral behavior.

Three of his former friends convinced Bill they should burglarize a house and steal a stereo. The homeowner caught them in the act and threatened to call the police if the would-be burglars didn't pay the damages for a broken door and return the stereo. Bill paid the damages and the woman kept her word not to report them to the police.

By this time Bill had worked his way into a managing position at David's buffet in Columbus. The compensation was less than what Bill thought it should be and he complained to the store manager. Bill had been involved in numerous arguments with his manager prior to the turnaround in his life. The manager had no confidence in the sincerity of Bill's decision. He suggested they sit down and drink. Bill's old desire for alcohol rekindled and he ended getting thoroughly drunk. He was seen by several of his friends in this condition and they made jokes about how short-lived his change was. Someone reported the incident to his pastor, Harold Smith.

Harold Smith was not only a lifesaver to Bill but a friend and mentor. When he learned of Bill's bout with alcohol, he didn't condemn him. He explained to those who made fun of Bill that a new Christian sometimes makes serious mistakes. Bill had made one and Harold confronted him by saying, "Bill, I see something in you. God will use you in a mighty way." Those words of encouragement and consistent instruction guided Bill through those first three years of his new freedom. During that time he learned how to share his encounter with Christ and the miraculous change he had experienced. He summed up the process in this way: "I had to put God first. I was a messed up believer in God. I had to learn to say, 'Lord, you got to help me. I'm afraid to be around Christians. I'm afraid I'll say or do something wrong. I'm afraid I'll spill my food. I'm afraid people won't believe me'." It was a difficult process but Bill's knowledge of God's love grew and his faith became rock solid. He came to the point of saying, "Lord, I'll let you have my life completely."

As a result of his commitment Bill began to find answers to his search for meaning and purpose in the Bible. He still struggled to read but he heard truths from the Bible from pastors and found them in the Bible. He found promises that gave him hope and peace. He believed God's promise to take care of his needs. Amazing things began to happen for him. When he lost his job at David's Buffet Bill moved into the room Westside Church offered him and paid them fifty dollars each month.

Before and After

66 **I** STARTED to learn more than I had ever learned before. I could remember things. I started to cook. I couldn't read recipes but I could remember them exactly.

"I got sick a few months after I was saved and went to Painesville, Ohio to be with my parents. The doctor warned me that my heart would give out if I didn't stop doing all the things I was doing as a Christian. God had a reason for my illness. My mother was saved about two months after I got home and then my sister and other family members. Some of my family was saved before I became a Christian. I really gave them a hard time because they had not told me how to become one before then. I could have died and gone to hell and they didn't tell me. I wasn't as kind to them as I should have been but in time our relationship improved until we became close. I went to visit my brother and a missionary led him to faith in Christ in Viet Nam. He was shocked at what had happened to me. I called him up in Viet Nam and told him about the Lord and sent him a letter. He bore no hard feelings toward me for the past. The Lord changed me so much that it got me into trouble. People I knew before I was a Christian would meet me and tell me they couldn't believe I was the same person they had known before."

"The more I understood the Christian life, the more I loved Jesus and the more He used me in reaching others. People I met and talked with would ask me what college I attended. I would introduce myself to college students in Columbus and share with them and they understood me. I could converse with them on a level they understood. I would pray and ask the Lord what words to say and He gave me the words to say. The only way I could explain it was the presence of God at work in my life as He promised in the Bible."

"I can remember days when I worked all day without an opportunity to speak with anyone about Christ. I would get on the bus in the evening and pray, 'Lord, it's almost midnight and you haven't used me. What's wrong?' And somehow the Lord would say to me, 'I'll use you.' One night I walked out the door of the bus and almost knocked a man down. I said, 'Lord, I couldn't catch him.' Sometimes I would have an opportunity to talk to someone and I didn't and I learned that person had died or been killed. It made me feel terrible. I know I talked with thousands of people about the Lord. I didn't preach at them although some may have thought I did."

"I went to the Painesville State Fair and over two hundred people accepted Christ. The first day of the fair, fourteen people I talked with accepted Christ as their Savior. The second day, twenty-one others made that decision. I found a friend who would go to the fair with me. I took some boxes with me. I would invite people to look inside the boxes. I would ask them if God could do anything. Most agreed God could do anything. Then I showed them one box that had written on it, 'Something God Can't Do.' When the box opened there was a picture of a casket and flowers and this Bible verse that said, 'God cannot let an unsaved person into heaven.' People would change their minds about God and about themselves. Another box would have the picture of a skeleton in it and this question, 'Where will you be when your body looks like this?' They would tell me, 'My body will be in the ground.' I would say to them, 'But, where will your soul be?' They would answer, 'I don't know.' I would ask them, 'Would you like to know the answer?' I would invite them to sit on a bench nearby and tell them about the Lord. I would give them a marked open Bible and ask them to read the underlined words. I would tell them my story how God changed my life and they would listen and over two hundred chose to follow Christ during State Fair that year."

"I met Bonnie and Clyde, motorcycle gang members. They belonged to the Outlaw gang in Columbus. Somebody told me about them and it scared me. I didn't want to go and see them but the Lord sent me. Clyde wasn't home but a friend of his led him to faith in Christ a short time later."

"I'm sad to say that there was some jealousy in my church because God used me to reach people where they were not effective. It was an inner city ministry and there were lots of opportunities and people to meet. A few wanted to put me on display for being effective but I wouldn't stand for it."

"Problems in the inner city of Columbus were so many that it was pathetic. One danger I faced was getting wrapped up in people's problems and letting it get to me. I learned to deal with people's problems the way the Lord made me see them and not the way other people saw them. I talked with a woman who had attempted suicide five times. I told her about Jesus and she told me it was the greatest thing that ever happened to her. She grabbed me and hugged me and kissed me. I talked to several other suicidal people. Some had razors but I talked them out of it. I talked to a lot of atheists. I had the joy of leading two of them to the Lord. Another man practiced black magic. We started our conversation at six in the morning and didn't finish until two-thirty the next morning. The entire time we were on the sidewalk. He knelt down finally on the sidewalk and turned from his ways to Christ. He was about twenty years old. The conversation started out with a gang of about ten boys. They all scattered except this one kid. Some of them would come back as we talked but only this one stayed. He would say that he wasn't ready to be saved. We would pray for him and he would say, 'Man, I've got to be saved!' Finally, he fell down on the sidewalk and prayed.

He went home and told his family, 'Don't laugh at me. I just got saved.' His brother said, 'What do you mean?' He said, 'Go out there and find out for yourself.' He came outside and was saved. I followed up on them for a long time. It was hard to see big changes in them because they came from such a messed up family."

"One man whom I shared with over the telephone is now a church staff worker in a church in North Columbus. An atheist I shared with moved out of the area and became active as a Christian in a church. I tried to follow up on anyone who became a Christian. I know how hard it is to understand what God has done for you when you're saved."

"I had a drinking problem before I was saved and did a lot of awful things. Folks would ask me, 'How can you be a Christian and talk about drinking?' I told them, 'God helped me overcome the drinking and I don't do that anymore.' They would say, 'That's impossible.' Nothing is impossible with God. He doesn't have to do it but He can do it. People would get angry at me when I witness to them. Here's how God used me in my life. People get mad and say God hasn't done that in my life. Well, this is what God has done in my life."

He's Still Working on Me

GOD took care of Bill's needs during his months of unemployment. Individuals continued to give Bill money during that time. Many said to him, "God told me to give this money to you." He never lacked for food or shelter during that time.

He was qualified to work in the food industry but no job opened. On his knees in prayer he asked God, "I need a job. I need a job right now." The next day Harold Smith came to his door and said, "Get dressed. I'm going to take you somewhere." They went to the Baptist Book Store. Harold Smith introduced Bill to Mrs. Anderson, the manager of the Book store. She interviewed Bill and asked him to tell her about his spiritual journey. She asked him if he had ever done any work like this before. He replied, "No, I never did anything like this." She was moved by his integrity and faith in God and asked him to pray about the job over the weekend and Monday morning if he still felt that God wanted him there he could come to work and the staff would help him work things out.

That weekend Bill prayed and prayed and felt led to accept the offer, even though he had never done anything like it before. He was sure that God would help him and show him how to handle the job.

Bill became a shipping clerk. He shipped packages all over the country. He learned the zip codes of the different states. He dealt with money, shipping, and orders. In his own way, he wrote down all of this. The meter he used gave him the prices to record and where they were shipped to and the Lord gave him the confidence to do it.

"I had no education. I learned very little at State School. I had some mental block and didn't learn. Only by the grace of God the Lord taught me to read and work. If the Lord had not taught me, I would not have made it. If God wanted me to learn computers then he would have shown me some way or somehow. Anything I did in life God would show me how to do it. You have to do it this way. I learned to trust the Lord. I had no other choice. I don't know recipes but The Lord said to me, 'Listen and watch because you are going to have to do this.' It amazed me. Whatever I did if the Lord was in it, He would tell me how to do it."

Every book has a code. That code would tell me where that book came from and what it was about and I learned what those codes meant and I knew. Everything seemed to come naturally to him. He would ask the staff to tell him zip code numbers. It was as if a camera clicked in his head and he remembered them. He knew it was God's hand at work in him.

Bill worked at the Baptist Book Store for the next seventeen years. The store changed managers and the managers changed the routine but they all told him, "You know shipping and you know receiving. When you get a package, write down what it is and check it into inventory." Since he couldn't read the invoices, Bill looked at the book. The back of the book had a code. Everything that came to the store had a code. Bill would look up that code and determine the identification of the book. The invoice would tell him the price and Bill would mark it accordingly.

There were daily shipments and each box had to be lifted and moved. Bill did it all. Each day there were truckloads to ship out. His familiarity with the stock led the management to send him to the sales floor to sell. Bill claimed that he could outsell anyone on the floor. He could not read a book but asked staff members to read books to him in the break room. People would ask him about a book. He would tell them, "Take the book home. Pay for it and take it home and read it and if you don't like it, send it back." No one ever sent back a book. Bill sold more than anyone. One pastor said to him, "You're selling me stuff I don't need." Bill's reply was, "Well,

I won't sell you something unless you need it." The customer laughed.

During the time Bill worked at Baptist Book Store he met numbers of pastors as well as other Christians. When he began work, an employee came to him and said, "You're going to find out that Christians aren't what they could be or should be." A few people told him that he should not be working or that he was not doing his job. His reply to each was, "Well, you didn't hire me. Mrs. Anderson did. She thinks I'm doing my job and if I have a problem she'll help me work it out." The complaints stopped. The number of complainers over the course of his tenure actually numbered only four individuals.

Word spread among churches in Ohio and across the States of this bold, young Christian working in a Baptist Book Store and leading more people to Christ than most pastors with their theological training. Churches and pastors began to invite Bill to share his faith with their congregations and challenge them to be bold witnesses for Christ.

Bill never advertised his willingness to share. People approached him at the book store and asked him to speak. He spoke for many years outside his own church. His speaking engagements led him to churches as far away as South Carolina, Tennessee, North Carolina and Florida. His work was featured in an article in Outreach Magazine and other periodicals. Who would ever have thought the angry, scared young teenager in Columbus State School would one day challenge audiences of hundreds to be bold witnesses of their faith in Christ? The only explanation Bill Reid gave was the greatness of God.

After seventeen years Bill had lifted so many boxes of books that his back was further weakened. One day he fell down a flight of stairs, cut his head open and ended up in the hospital for two weeks. He remembered hitting the bottom step thinking, "Lord, now what do you have in store for me?" The Bible says, "…all things work together for good to those who love God, to those who are called according to His purpose." (Romans 8:27-29) God had more work for Bill Reid.

The hospital report included three broken ribs on each side and a deep cut to his scalp. The store manager visited him and encouraged him. "Don't worry about it. Your salary will continue. Get well. Maybe God has something in store for you here."

About three o'clock in the morning a man was assigned the bed next to his. He was in his late seventies. He was a black man and had suffered a stroke. Bill could hear him trying to talk and once again God impressed him that this was why he was here. That really excited him. He started to ask God for an opportunity to talk to his roommate. The next day the man's family came into the room and Bill let them know that he was a Christian. They told him, "We've been trying to talk to our Dad for years and he will not listen to what we tell him about God. Maybe you can talk to him."

The two roommates became friends over the next week and a half. Bill knew he was going to be released and said to the man, "Did you know that God loves you? Did you know God died for you? Would you like to know Him in a personal way?" He said, "Yes." They both got down on hands and knees by the bed and the man accepted Christ as his personal Lord and Savior. Both men were rejoicing, hugging each other, talking about Jesus. Bill said, "Now, tomorrow when you wake up, call your family and tell them what happened to you." He did and they came to see him that day and expressed their joy to Bill for his help. He knew again that God had placed him in this circumstance for a reason and he had been faithful to serve Him.

Friends on the Outside

FOR someone to be as violent and uncontrollable as Billy Reid for twenty-five years and then to gain the admiration and respect of so many friends and acquaintances for the next forty years is rare. These friends and acquaintances paint an entirely different picture of him after his encounter with Christ. The observation of V.J. Sanchez who knew Bill for a period of thirty-five years following his experiences at State School is typical of those who met and knew him.

"My niece was president of her youth group at St. Matthew's Lutheran Church in Logan, Ohio. She called to ask if I knew someone who had an unusual encounter with God that changed him greatly. Her youth group was having a retreat and she wanted someone to share a life-changing encounter with God. She didn't know anyone in her church she could ask to share."

"I called a member of the Briggs Road Baptist Church in Columbus, a church my wife and I had recently joined. One of the members suggested Bill Reid. She gave me a brief sketch of him and his phone number. I called Bill and explained my niece's request. He said that he would be glad to share with them. I made arrangements to pick him up and take him to Logan, Ohio to share with the group."

"What Billy told them was incredible! Most of the people at the retreat had never heard a story like his. Actually, several of the youth leaders challenged Billy about his personal experience with God. He remained calm and answered their questions respectfully but firmly."

"I was impressed more with Billy's answers to their challenges than with his life story, which was amazing in itself. That was the start of a great friendship with Billy Reid which I cherish."

Debbi first became acquainted with Bill Reid when she was a teenager living in a poorer section of Columbus. She recalled, "The adults in our neighborhood told all of us that Billy was crazy. 'Stay away from him!' The way he struggled with every movement to walk fascinated me as a teen. He seemed to put so much effort and physical exertion into moving. I saw him walking everywhere in our neighborhood. I knew he didn't have a car because there was no way for him physically to drive."

"When I graduated from high school my parents moved from 'the bottoms' to 'the hilltop' and I lost track of Billy. It was several years later than my new husband and I began to attend a church and met Bill and Sheena there. As I watched and learned of his accomplishments I realized what an extraordinary person he was."

"The bits and pieces Bill shared about the way he grew up brought tears to my eyes. Eventually, I learned he could not read or write. I found that to be unbelievable because he worked at the Baptist Book Store as their shipping clerk. How could a person who can't read or write possibly fill orders and ship them across the country. When I asked Billy about it he said, 'I memorize the codes on the back of each book and that tells me what the book is and where it goes. I ask people to read books to me during lunch breaks and that tells me what's in them.' I'm still amazed that he was able to do what he did there."

"Several years after I met Bill I became certified to teach adults to read and write. I thought of Bill and determined that he would be my first 'victim' to teach. My office wasn't far from where he lived, so I would go on my lunch break to teach Bill. I soon realized that Bill had some dyslexic needs and other learning disabilities that I was not trained to treat. We both did our best but I didn't succeed in teaching him to read or write. I felt I had failed a good friend but Bill wasn't upset.

He just shrugged his shoulders and said, 'God must not want me to learn to read and write.'"

"I've known Bill for over twenty-five years and I still marvel at the work that God has started and is continuing to do in and through him. Bill has been through dozens of physical, spiritual and emotional setbacks but in his true fashion, he always gives God the credit and praise for guiding him through each one. He's an amazing and inspiring creation of God. I've been blessed to know him and call him my friend."

Bill prayed for people to change and God changed them. He also prayed for God to provide needs in his own life and God provided. Myla Cullen recounts her first meeting with Bill Reid. It was on a cold Ohio winter night at Saint Anns Hospital. She was leaving the hospital and saw Bill waiting in the cold for a bus to take him home. She said to him, "You're not going to take a bus. I'm going to give you a ride home. It's way too cold to stand here and wait for a bus." Bill had forgotten to call his wife.

"That was the first time I met his beautiful wife, Sheena, and I must say the first thing I noticed was her clean, orderly home. Since then our friendship has grown. I got to know their lovely children, William and Rebecca. Bill is a godly man. He always places God first in his life. He has a lot of faith and trusts in God for everything. Sometimes I chuckle at how much Bill trusts God to provide. He kept telling me he was going to get a hot tub. Oh, did he pray for that hot tub! He kept telling me that God would supply his need. Several months passed and our pastor called Bill to ask him if he wanted a hot tub. Of course, Bill told him, 'Yes!' and thanked God for answering his prayer. Bill Reid is a special friend."

Paul and Sally Adkins recalled their first meeting with Bill Reid in 1965. Bill had only become a Christian a few months earlier, but already demonstrated a positive and loving attitude toward others. They said, "He was so in love with the Lord that he wanted everyone he met to know his Lord. He was full of joy for the Lord. In the forty years we've known him he has always reached out to people less fortunate than himself. He looks for ways to help them and share his life-changing faith with them in a positive manner. I've never known him and his wife, Sheena, not to have someone living with them. They are always providing a place for anyone in need. It has been a joy and privilege to know Bill and his family over these years."

Myla Cullen was staying with friends in the neighborhood where Bill lived. Myla's friend, Grandma Johnson asked Bill to take care of Myla if anything should happen to her. Of course he and Sheena agreed. How did they feel about the arrangement? Bill told a friend, "Myla has been a blessing. She helps Sheena and me spiritually and financially. She's such a blessing. We can talk with her about the Lord, about our problems and she understands. Myla loves the Lord more than anything else. She had suffered through cancer and the

Lord healed her. She had bad eyesight but she continually encourages us. She trusts God no matter what happens knowing that He will work things out for good. I thank God for Myla Cullen and hope she can continue living with us."

When Myla became homeless, Bill and Sheena brought her home to live with them. As both of them say, "She has been a blessing to us. She's a committed Christian, committed to the Lord more than anything else. She's been through cancer and other circumstances. She trusts in God to work things out. Myla is one of those who have lived in our home through our thirty years of marriage."

The Bill Reid known by his friends and neighbors in Columbus, Ohio is a far different person than the troubled teen who came to Columbus State School and the bitter young man who left there eight years later.

Sheena's Wedding

Bill and Sheena

WHEN Bill was twelve years old his mother told him, "Some day, you're going to marry a girl and the two of you will have a girl and a boy. You will drive a car." His sister, Dorothy, told him that he should never marry and never drive a car. He didn't pay any attention to his sister but often wondered about his mother's prediction. Whenever he was challenged, Bill always had to prove the challenger wrong and on his sister's prediction, he did.

Bill thought about finding a larger church to attend. In conversation with Harold Smith, his pastor, Bill observed, "You know, it seems like there are no girls my age that I would like to be around or go out with. It just seems that most of them have a lot of problems of their own." Harold replied, "Bill, some day a girl will come in that door and you'll look at her and that will be your wife."

Bill was now thirty-seven years old. His brief attempt at marriage at age twenty-seven had failed. Sure enough, six months after his pastor's encouragement Sheena came in the door of the church building and God touched Bill's heart.

"There's your wife," I thought. Bill did some serious praying. "Lord, if she's not a Christian, I won't go with her until she becomes one." Two weeks later, Sheena did accept Christ and she and Bill became very good friends. Six months later, the two were married. It was a marriage made in heaven. A year later their first son was born and named after his father, William Gary Reid. Bill had found his soul-mate.

Sheena was ten years younger and had experienced some of the same rejection and abandonment Bill had known. She and Bill had some of the same issues and circumstances. They understood each other. They were a completed couple.

"We've had our ups and downs," Sheena recalled, "but through God we've been blessed. We're growing in the Lord every day. We've been together almost thirty years. I wasn't a good person when I met Billy. I visited Westside Church after a friend invited me to worship there. I had pretty much given up on churches and God by that time. I was born in St. Mary's, Ohio on the other side of Ohio from Columbus. I lived there with my parents and a brother and sister in my early childhood. I went to school there. During my high school years, Dad moved us to Indiana. He bought a new house but my mother missed her family in Ohio so much that we sold the house and moved back to Ohio. Mom and Dad started having marital problems. Mom met this guy, Robert, and she divorced my Dad. My Dad was very depressed. He tried to kill himself because of the situation with my Mom.

"Later, my Dad met another woman. He told her he had three kids, but She didn't want anything to do with us. By then, my brother was old enough to move out. Dad hired a woman to stay with my sister and me. When I was fifteen years old Dad packed me and my sister up and sent us to Pennsylvania to live with my Mom and her boyfriend, Robert. He had a tree trimming business and I went to work for him. It was a rough time. We moved back to Ohio. My Dad had married in the meantime. His wife was named Martha. She and Dad lived for a while in Columbus, Ohio. Mom married Woody and moved to Tennessee with my sister and me. We lived with Mom and Woody for a few years. Mom had two more kids, Bobbie and Sue. I stayed around and watched them while Mom and Woody worked. I moved a lot. I had little education. I spent most of my younger years taking care of my family.

"I met Billy at Westside Baptist Church. He came through the back door of the church the same time I came through the front door. My sister introduced me to him at the close of the worship service and he sat down next to my father. We talked a few minutes and that week Billy showed up at my sister's house with a half-gallon of ice cream for her two small girls. Billy wasn't very subtle but he was persistent about what he wanted. We talked a while and Billy said that he had to leave. I asked him if he needed a ride and he said, 'I'll take the bus. That's how I get around town.' Since it was getting late, I offered to drop him off at his house and he accepted my offer. The following Sunday Billy asked if I would have lunch with him. I agreed to go but I was nervous about the whole matter. I remember thinking, 'I hope this isn't leading up to anything.' I really didn't want to hurt Bill's feelings. He really was a nice guy. One thing led to another and before long Bill asked me to marry him. Six months later we were planning a wedding. We were married in August 1981. Every time I've been discouraged, Billy has picked me up . He always tells me that God loves me. After we married, we lived in a small house. Woody was sick and he and Mom came to live with us until Woody went to a rest home. Mom lived with us for twenty years until she became sick and died. We took care of her all that time. My Dad and Martha moved in with us after Woody and Mom until Dad got sick. Shortly before he died, he and Martha found a place to live. After he died, Martha went to live with her daughters. "

"My brother Bobby was living with a girl and had two kids. The two split up and Bobby met another girl who was an alcoholic. My brother had become an alcoholic, too. He lost his kids to their mother and became homeless. Billy and I tried to help him but four years later, he died from bacterial meningitis, the result of eating out of trash cans and drinking himself to death. He died on a couch in a friend's house. We had him cremated and his sister took his ashes home with her.

My life has been no bed of roses. I constantly moved around and cared for family and friends."

"Billy and I have always had someone living with us. We have never really lived alone. We've always tried to care for people. Billy is beginning to weaken from his cerebral palsy, but he keeps on going. Now, my sister is living with us downstairs."

"I've suffered with sugar diabetes, thyroid problems, high cholesterol, and a failed operation that left a hernia. I've had six hernias and another is beginning. That's the story of my life and how God changed me from the person I was. My life changed tremendously when I married Billy. Billy has been an inspiration to me and my family by his walk with the Lord. Our thirty years of marriage couldn't have been better. If I hadn't met him I don't know where I would be today. I just praise God for what He has done in my life. We're living the best that we can."

"When I met Billy I ran around and did things I now regret. The Lord saved me and changed me. If He would do that for me and for Billy, I know He can do it for anyone."

"Our daughter, Rebecca, was born and named by Bill's mother after the Rebecca in the Bible. Both our children attended church growing up. If the church door opened, they were there. Both accepted Christ as their personal Savior at an early age. As many young Christians do, both of them explored life outside of church but came back to the strong faith we have."

"After the children were grown, Pastor Harold Smith retired from Westside Baptist Church. Bill had attended since his conversion. Now, he felt we should look for a church where we would be welcome, one where we could continue to grow in Christ. We were invited to lots of neighboring churches. Bill insisted that the only church he would attend had to be the one God led him to join."

"We were driving through town looking for a church, and God spoke to Bill. Bill said, 'Turn the car around. Go to Briggs Road Baptist Church. This is where God wants us to be.' So, I turned the car in the opposite direction and found Briggs Road Church. Two weeks later we joined that church. Shortly after we joined, the pastor announced his resignation and the church was left without a pastor."

The church decided together to ask Rev. Ron Hopkins to be their new pastor. In typical Baptist fashion, each church member voted either yes or no whether to call the new pastor. Bill and Sheena were in the congregation for the vote. When Bill marked his ballot, "No," Sheena whispered to him, "Billy, what are you doing? You like Pastor Hopkins." Bill whispered to her, "I do like him. I want him to be our pastor, but God just told me to vote no." Bill and Sheena had been praying together for the church to call a pastor. They had asked God to allow Ron Hopkins to be their pastor. But, that morning,

Bill was impressed in his spirit that he should vote, "No." And, he did."

"I was being obedient to God," Bill said. "Something told me to say 'no.'" The church called the pastor in spite of Bill's "no" vote. The church grew rapidly under Pastor Hopkin's leadership and Bill felt badly that he said "no." He wanted him to come as pastor but felt he had to vote "no." The pastor accepted the invitation of the congregation and came as their pastor. Bill felt badly that his was the only negative vote among the congregation that morning. Six months later Bill was walking through the church building when the pastor walked into the room. Bill began to cry and the pastor asked, "What's wrong?" Bill said, "Pastor, I didn't vote for you. I don't know why I didn't vote for you. I wanted you to be our pastor but I felt I had to vote, 'No'."

"The pastor hugged Bill and said, 'Billy, you are the only person who didn't vote for me to come as pastor. My wife and I prayed that one person would vote no. If more than one voted no we would not come. You were obedient to God and did what God told you to do. I was very happy you voted 'no'. That's how I knew we were to agree to serve this church as pastor. If there had been two, I would not have come to Briggs Road Church. But, there was one and that's why I came, because you were obedient to God and did what God wanted you to do.' Bill was overjoyed! He had closure for his strange response in the church vote. He had not mistaken God's direction. He had voted, "No!"

Again and again, Bill demonstrated his intimate relationship with God. One moment, he had no belief in God and no desire to live. The next moment, he had a personal relationship with a loving God that guided him through each day for the rest of his life.

Bill, Sheena and William

Spreading the Good News

Bill's desire to tell people about Christ and see them turn to Him as Savior was apparent. If he heard that someone was dying, his first thought was whether or not they knew about Christ. He was deeply concerned to find an opportunity to talk with them.

People often called Bill to intervene in the lives of their friends and family who had reached the end of their hope. One woman called and asked him to go to a hospital and talk to a girl who had attempted suicide. The girl had drunk a bottle of bleach and swallowed pills. She had been distraught over a breakup with her boyfriend. Her attempt had left her in a coma.

Bill agreed to visit her the next day. During the night, a recurring back injury left him barely able to move. When he awoke, Bill asked God, "Lord, if You want me to see this girl, You'll have to deal with my back. I can hardly walk." He called his daughter who was living with them at home and asked, "Will you take me to the hospital. I need to see a girl who's in a coma. She may not live very long. I want to see if I can do something for her." Bill felt deeply that God wanted him to go.

His daughter said, "Daddy, you can't go in this condition." Bill said, "Don't worry about it. The Lord will work it out." As he got into the car, the pain increased. He determined to go and promised his daughter if he had any further problem, he would call her to come for him. The moment Bill walked through the hospital door, the pain went away. All of it! Bill said, "I knew the Lord was in this." He found the room and asked to see the patient. Her name was Barbara. Bill remembered fondly calling her, "Bobbie Lou" when she was a small girl. Her family used that same name for her. Bobbie Lou was one of the children of Bill's first wife.

The nurse on duty explained that Barbara was in an intensive care unit. No one but the hospital staff could see her. Bill related to the nurse that Barbara's family had asked him to visit her and he was part of the visitation team from Briggs Road Church. The nurse nodded and said, "If the staff will let you into her room, you can go."

As Bill stepped off the elevator in front of the intensive care unit, all the doors to the unit were open. The nurse downstairs had given him the room number and Bill walked into the intensive care unit and into her room.

A nurse was attending Barbara and asked what he wanted. Bill told her that the family had asked him to come and pray for their daughter. The nurse told him he could. Bill took Barbara by the hand and prayed a silent prayer. "Lord, show me what to say because I don't know what to say to a person in a coma. Help Bobbie Lou to hear what I tell her and respond to it." As he started to pray aloud, Bill heard God say to him, "Billy, tell her that this is her last opportunity to come to know God. She will have no other opportunity." Bill said, "I looked up and said, 'Who said that?'" The nurse said, "What are you talking about?" I said, "I don't know but somebody said something to me." He bowed his head and started to pray again and the Lord spoke to him again and said, "Tell her this is her last opportunity to be saved." Bill said to Bobbie Lou, "I'm saying to you what God told me to say. He told me this is your last opportunity to come to know Christ as your Savior." Bill kept repeating those words to her, "This is your last opportunity." He glanced up and the nurse was looking at him very agitated, but he kept repeating the words again and again.

Then, Barbara's eyes started blinking. Her feet began to move and she began to move her arms and came out of the coma and said to Bill, "Billy, this is my last opportunity to come to Christ." The nurse flipped out! She ran out of the room and called, "Doctor! Doctor! Come see!" The doctor ran in and said, "Everybody, get out!" I said, "Oh no, I won't have an opportunity to talk to her." The doctor said, "I'm saying, everybody out!" As Bill walked down the hallway, Barbara's boyfriend walked up behind him. Bill turned to him and said, "God told me to tell you this is your last opportunity to be saved." He shared with the young man how to have a personal relationship with Christ. The boy kept walking and Bill walked with him. Whemun they reached the elevator the boy said to Bill, "I have to see someone."

The elevator stopped operating. So, Bill continued to talk to the young man. "God is telling me you need to be saved. You need to repent of your sin. You need to know Jesus." People waiting for the elevator were listening to this conversation.

Bill turned to his growing audience and continued to share with them how they might have a life-changing encounter with God in Christ. By the time the elevator began to operate again fifteen people were standing around Bill. The boy said, "I'm not ready to be saved." Bill said, "God told me to tell you this is your last opportunity." He said, "I have to go." At that moment, the elevator door opened and the boy left.

Before leaving, Bill asked, "Lord, am I finished? I tried to talk to Barbara. I tried to talk to her boyfriend. Now what do you want me to do?" Again the Lord spoke to him, "Bill stand still and I'll show you." As Bill stood there he overheard a woman talking on her cell phone. She was saying, "My daughter is going to die!" That caught his attention. As she moved toward Bill, her grandmother came toward her saying,

"We need someone to pray." The ladies who had been standing nearby said to Bill, "You can pray." So, Bill began to pray. Afterward, he shared with the women. They thanked him for his prayer and for sharing with them how they could have peace with God.

Another man came into the waiting area and said, "I'm looking for my Dad. My son, his grandson, is about to die." Bill said to him, "Can I pray?" He asked Bill if he would. As he prayed again, another group of people listened.

All in all, it had been an interesting day in the life of Bill Reid. A year later Bill learned that Bobbie Lou had been killed in a car-truck accident and her husband was in the hospital in critical condition.

Bill had a neighbor who was not a Christian. He often sat on his front porch with two large dogs. One was a German Shepherd and the other a mixed Shepherd dog. The German Shepherd dog didn't like Bill and he was afraid of dogs to start with. God would tell Bill to talk to his neighbor about the Lord. Bill would say, "Not today, Lord, maybe tomorrow." Tomorrow came and Bill would say, "Not today." Several weeks passed and Bill's brother came home one night and asked him if he had heard the news that the neighbor died. "It was like a bolt of lightning through my body," Bill said. "I should have shared Christ but day after day I went by with my eyes closed. I can see him now on that porch and hear God telling me to talk to him about Jesus. I keep telling people about him hoping they will listen when God tells them to share the Gospel with another. It may be the last opportunity they have to hear and you may be the last person they have to tell them."

From the first moment of his own dramatic conversion, Bill wanted to tell everyone he could about the change Jesus Christ brought to him. When he got on a bus to travel, he would pray that God would send someone to sit beside him who needed to know the Lord. When he got off the bus he would look for someone else to share with. Some believed and some did not.

"I went to a friend's house and he invited me to meet some people. I met a Christian man and he said, 'Let's talk a minute.' He had these small boxes, about five. 'Look in one of them and tell me what you think. Prettiest flowers you will ever see. Always remember to give people flowers before they die.' The next box held bones. 'Where will you be when your body looks like this?' 'I'll be dead.' 'No. Your body will be dead but your spirit within you is real. Let me show you where you could be.' The next box had a scripture that explained how to have a home in heaven. He gave me these boxes and I took them to the Ohio State Fair and showed them to hundreds of people. Some believed and some did not."

Bill prayed about day to day concerns. After several years of marriage, he and Sheena decided to buy a house. A friend recommended a realtor who led them through the process to find the right house. Bill prayed for a house in an area where God would use him to introduce neighbors to Christ. They found the house they wanted, but there was one huge obstacle. Three thousand dollars was needed for closing fees. Bill didn't have the money. He started to pray. He asked God to provide the money needed. A few days passed and a check arrived from the Internal Revenue Service. The amount of the check was three thousand dollars. Bill knew once more that the Lord was guiding him. The house had five bedrooms and a three car garage, but Sheena didn't like it. Bill convinced her that her ability to decorate would change her mind and she did.

Everyone in Bill's neighborhood knew that he was a Christian. He didn't push his belief upon them. He simply prayed and waited for God to arrange opportunities to tell people his story. Bill understood the power of prayer as few Christians do. He depended upon prayer to provide his needs and the needs of others.

One of these was a neighbor whose wife was hospitalized in a coma. The man would visit her every Sunday and Bill tried time after time to talk to this man about his relationship to God. He talked to him over a period of ten years. He was unable to get anywhere with him. One day Bill learned the man was in the hospital suffering from a bad heart condition. Bill went to visit him and again shared his faith in Christ with him. His neighbor accepted Christ and thanked Bill for sharing with him. Three days later the neighbor died. The man who hated God and had no interest in spiritual things had become an obedient follower of Christ who shared his faith effectively with people around him.

Some of Bill's neighbors sent people they knew to see Bill. They would tell their friends, "Bill's a Christian. You need to talk to him." Bill would share Christ with them and lead them to Christ.

Bill's son and daughter would bring their young friends home and Bill would share Christ with them. At times this upset them and Bill would explain, "I can't help it. The Lord tells me to do something and I have to do it." He was effective in leading some of these kids to a life-changing encounter with Christ. He respected the kids and they had a lot of respect for Bill.

Prayer opened opportunities. A neighbor living a few houses from Bill and Sheena told Bill about his heartaches and he had many. Bill often shared his faith. His twenty-year-old son was struck by a drunken driver and left in a vegetative state. The father became an alcoholic and drank all the time. Bill shared his experiences with the Lord with the man and his friends. His friends responded with profanity and vulgarity to irritate Bill. The neighbor asked Bill repeatedly, "How can God love us and do this to my son?" Bill explained to him that God didn't do this, the devil did." Bill continued to talk to him.

One day the man said, "Billy, I don't want you to talk to me about the Lord ever again. I'm just sick of it." So Bill replied, "Okay, I won't talk to you any more about the Lord." The next day, Bill went to his house and borrowed some tools to work on a car. A friend of Bill's named Billy Watkins came over to help him. The neighbor showed up and it was evident he had been drinking and was agitated. Bill didn't say anything to him about the Lord, so he was civil, until Bill broke one of his tools and he became angry. Bill gave him the broken tool and promised to replace it or pay him for it.

The next day the neighbor knocked on Bill's door and said, "I want all my tools back." He cursed Bill in the process and Bill lost his temper. He gathered up the tools, took them over to the man's place and threw them down in front of his garage. Bad mistake! The neighbor came out of his garage and ran at Bill calling him every name in his vocabulary and threatening to kill him. Bill was so scared he admitted later he would have shot the man if he had a gun. "I never want to see you again. I never want to talk to you and if I do, I'll beat you up. I'll kill you," the man raged. Bill was wise enough to keep his mouth shut. Under his old nature, he would have been fighting. He was shaking when he went home. Sheena opened the door and said, "What's wrong with you?" Bill replied, "I don't want to talk to you. I don't want to talk to anybody. I just need to settle down." Sheena continued, "What happened?" Bill said, "I can't tell you." He went into his bedroom to hide his shaking.

He was scared because this man was a neighbor. He knew he would eventually come into contact with him again. He really was afraid of what would happen. Sheena and Bill's son were both angry about the incident. His son threatened to confront the man and whip him, if necessary. He said, "Nobody does that to my dad." Bill demanded that he not say or do anything. He said, "I have to deal with this myself. Not you or anybody else, not even my friend, Billy Watkins, can do anything. Billy Watkins threatened to beat the neighbor up. Bill said, "You can't do that. I'll deal with him."

Three months passed and Bill met the irate neighbor at the trash can. He looked at Bill and Bill said, "Hi." The man said, "Hi. I'm sorry for what I said. Please forgive me." Afterward they became best friends. Even though he hasn't accepted Christ or stopped his drinking, they remain good friends and Bill continues to pray for an opportunity to introduce him to Jesus Christ.

Since Bill had difficulty driving, he rode the bus most of the time. He would get on a bus and say to God, "God, do You want me to talk to that person over there? Have that person either come over and sit beside me or turn to me and I know this is what you want me to do."

Often bus riders would get up from their seat and move over to sit beside Bill. They would start to talk about their troubles and Bill would say to them. "You know, we all have problems and I have a solution to your troubles. That's Jesus.

I know he can save you. I know He can help you. I know because He loves me and He helped me." Leading people to a life-changing encounter with Christ was not unusual for Bill.

"If you feel sorry for yourself God won't use you. I was sitting on a bus and people on the bus were making fun of me by the way I walk and talk. Three grown men bigger than me were laughing the most. God said to me, 'Let me do the talking through you.' I told them, 'I know you are laughing at me. What bothers me is not that you are laughing at me but someday you may have a child that is just like me. Will you love it or laugh at it like you are laughing at me?' Those guys turned purple."

Not everyone appreciated Bill's boldness and faith. In fact, some of the people in Bill's church would get upset with him because he would bring people, all kinds of people, into the worship services. But, many of them would find Christ and their lives would change. Others could see the change in them.

After the turn around in Bill's life he did everything he dreamed of doing as a troubled child but could not until he put his trust in God and God helped him. He married. He drove a car. He had children. He had a purpose for living joyfully.

Another Miracle

BILL'S first memories of his father were associated with alcohol. His father was a heavy drinker and continued to drink heavily into his last years. Bill could not remember his father ever telling him that he loved him. If he did tell him, Bill never remembered.

After the change in his life, Bill heard the Lord telling him, "I want you to go home and talk to your Dad about Me." Bill objected. He was scared of his father. His father was always drunk. Finally, the Lord let Bill get sick enough that he had to go home to recover. He lived with his parents in Mountville, Ohio for three and a half years.

In his father's house, Bill started to pray for his Dad. He prayed for quite a long time. He asked his pastor to pray for his Dad. Bill's father hated preachers. In fact, he would verbally run preachers away from his home. He never went to church. He might have gone to a church when he was a child but nothing happened to make a difference in his life as an adult.

Sitting at a table with his Dad, Bill started to share his faith with him. His Dad looked across the table and said, "I want to kill you." He picked up a knife and came around the table toward Bill. As his Dad picked up the knife, Bill began to pray silently. "Lord, You're going to have to intervene in some way. Somehow You're going to have to intervene." Bill stood up beside the table and said to his Dad, "The Lord's not going to let you hurt me." His Dad took three steps and fell down, blinded. He couldn't see. Bill took the knife from him.

His Dad said, "I don't know where I am. I'm in total darkness and there's fire all around me. I don't know what's happening and I don't like it." He yelled a few times and Bill and his sister picked him up and put him into bed. Bill said to Ruth, his sister, "I believe God is showing Dad what hell is." His Dad didn't believe in hell. He didn't believe in heaven. He believed that you die and that's it.

After three days, Bill's Dad regained his sight. Bill realized that God was using this situation for him to talk to his father. He had asked God to open a door, a way to talk to his father, and God gave him one. A few months passed. Bill had regained his health and gone to look for a job when his mother called him and said, "Your Dad had a dream. He asked me to get him a piece of paper to write his will because he felt he was going to die."

Mrs. Reid was gone several minutes looking for a piece of paper. When she returned to Mr. Reid, he had tears in his eyes. He was crying. He said, "I died and my mother was with me and took my hand and we went through the ceiling, and up to the clouds; we went to the stars, past the moon and sun. We went to a large gate. The gate opened and a bright light shined and a voice said to me, 'Why should I let you into my Kingdom?' When I heard the voice say that, I came back into my body." His wife asked, "What did you see?" He said, "I don't want to talk about it." But she said, "I know what you saw. You saw the Lord's glory."

For several days, Mr. Reid wouldn't talk about the incident. Mrs. Reid called Bill to tell him, she was certain God wanted Bill to talk to his father again. Bill came home and when he was alone with his Dad he began to pray silently, "Lord, show me something to know when You want me to talk to Dad about Jesus."

His father said, "I wish I was dead. I don't want to live anymore." Bill spoke to his Dad, "If you did die, where would you go?" He said, "Well, when you die, you're dead and that's it." Bill replied, "Okay, let's look at it this way. Suppose you die and nothing...there's nothing...you're dead. You don't have anything to lose, but suppose you're wrong. Suppose there's a heaven, suppose there's a hell, where would you go?"

He said, "I don't know." Then Bill reminded him of the dream his Dad saw and the darkness he experienced and continued, "God is trying to show you there's a hell and through this dream, God is trying to show you heaven. You have to make the choice. You have to accept Christ as your personal Savior and be forgiven your sin. You have to repent of your sin."

Mr. Reid reacted. "I want to get out of here. I don't want to talk about this." Bill pressed the issue. "Dad, you have no choice, but the Lord wants me to tell you that He loves you and He died for you. He wants to save you."

Mr. Reid's face reacted in frustration. He tried to get out of his chair but couldn't stand. Bill repeated, "God's not going to let you out of that chair until I tell you how to be saved." Then, Bill carefully explained to his Dad what he needed to understand to find peace with God. At that point he gave him another opportunity to accept or reject Christ.

Mr. Reid blurted, "I don't want to talk about it. I don't want to talk about it." Bill relented. "Okay." "I don't want you to tell me anymore about God," Mr. Reid went on. And Bill half-heartedly agreed, "Okay, I won't." Then his Dad yelled for Mrs. Reid. "Billy's talking to me about God! I don't want to talk about God! She said, "You better listen to what he's saying before its too late." The conversation ended on that note.

A few years later, Pastor Harold Smith told Bill he was going to Akron, Ohio for a meeting. Bill asked him, "Will you go see my Dad?" Harold Smith had met Mr. Reid before but never really talked about God. Mr. Reid liked Harold Smith. He went to see him.

Mrs. Reid was with her husband and during the visit Harold Smith asked her to leave so that he could talk to Mr. Reid. So, she and the pastor's wife left the room. This time Bill's Dad was receptive to the invitation to accept Christ and asked God to forgive him and come into his life and change his life as He had Billy's life.

Harold called Bill and told him the news. Bill could hardly believe it. To himself he said, "I have to see this for myself." A few days later he went to see his Dad. The change in him was apparent. For the first time in his life, Bill and his Dad talked about spiritual things together. Three days later, Mr. Reid had a major stroke. He could no longer walk. He could speak very little. He lived in this condition for another thirteen years before he died. Bill's sister, Ruth, talked to her dad several times after the stroke about his relationship with Christ. Mr. Reid was unable to respond, except to weep openly. Bill continued to rejoice in his Dad's belated decision and the obvious change he saw in him before his stroke and death. Once again, God had been merciful. Once again, God chose to use the man whom everyone else had given up on to be part of what God alone can do. Another miracle had taken place.

The Family

BILL'S family was a great source of encouragement to him after his conversion. Esther lived until she was eighty and had come to love Jesus deeply. She was very prayerful in her later years. She was saved in 1953 before Bill went to State School. Betty and Bill were together with their mother when she died. "We could hear the angels of heaven," Bill recalled.

Johnny, one of Bill's older brothers helped him in times of need. The two of them often discussed the Bible after Bill's conversion.

George was a good friend and brother. Bill remembered the Christmas in his childhood when George bought the boys a sled.

The baby, Raymond, died when he was three months old. Bill remembered his Mother's grief when baby Raymond died. "She was very upset and cried a lot and couldn't contain herself. Later on she told me she was in the bedroom crying when the Lord came to her and she saw her mother and baby in heaven. He was in the hands of Jesus. After that she didn't cry or worry anymore."

Esther would wait up for Billy and Donald when they sneaked out at night. She would always say, "I'm glad you're home." Once, on a brief visit home, Don and Billy stole their sister's car and took it for a drive. Billy was seventeen at the time and Don only fifteen. They were driving across a railroad track and the car stopped. A train came and was only five feet from them when they got the car across the track.

Bill's brother, Allen, moved to California. Bill and the rest of the family knew very little about him. They lost contact with him after his move.

Bill described his sister, Barbara, as one of the most dedicated Christians he knew. When the Lord sent Bill home to talk to his family she told him, "Maybe someday, I will be saved." One day she prayed on her way to pick Bill up, "I hope Billy won't talk to me about God," she thought. God told her, "Don't pray that." Barbara turned to Christ and found the joy her brother knew. She raised eight kids. Barbara had a habit of making a cup of tea for herself and the Lord when she was praying. On one occasion she noticed some of the tea was gone from the cup. Her first thought was that the Lord drank it.

The furnace in the basement where she lived had a habit of backfiring and filling the room with smoke. Barbara went to the basement where the furnace was and prayed that it would not backfire and cover her with smoke again. It never backfired again. She often called Bill and told him what the Lord had done for her. She flew to California to visit her dying daughter. The plane was in a bad storm and she prayed for protection. She felt His Presence. She looked out the window and saw four angels holding up the wings of the plane. People came and sat beside her when they saw her praying because they felt the Lord was with her.

Bill's recollections of Dorothy were fond. Dorothy remembered being in church when the Lord's Supper was being served. She was young and someone told her she should not take if because she was not saved. She was so concerned because no one told her how to be saved. It was many years later that she became a Christian.

Bill's brother, Lewis, was a strong Christian. He was saved about seven years before Bill. He told Bill he had been saved those seven years and Bill really "chewed him out" because he had not told him how to be saved. Lewis apologized. Now, the two are good friends. He is an encourager for his brother.

Don was the one who got into so many fights with Billy. He was involved in most of the trouble Billy got into at home. Billy was insanely jealous of him. He could do things Billy couldn't do. The privileges he had which Billy didn't have made Billy jealous and bitter. He could ride the lawnmower and Billy could not. No one explained to Billy why he could not do things. All of this made him angry.

Ruth was Bill's younger sister. She also is a Christian now. The two read the Bible together after her salvation. "I remember throwing cigarettes on my brother's car and while my sister and younger brother were in the car playing. My cigarettes ignited the car. My Dad yelled, 'Fire!' I ran downstairs and my Dad yelled, 'Where are the kids'? Ruth and my nephew were in the fire and both got out. They were in the chicken house where the car was parked. I didn't tell my family until after I was saved that I was the one who nearly burned them to death."

Have Things Changed?

A FORMER director of nursing in an Ohio developmental center similar to State School where Bill was a resident, related the need for more change in the care of emotionally disturbed and physically challenged children state-wide. Her psychiatric nursing background and experience growing up with a family member with Down's Syndrome gave her a compelling reason to seek employment in the field of nursing.

She described several instances of abusive treatment of disabled residents she witnessed in an institution run by the state. "During my first year, I learned from other members of management that they never went to one particular cottage because they were 'afraid' of what they might witness. I really couldn't believe it!"[4]

For reporting abuses and expressing concerns for the welfare of the residents, this director was placed on administrative leave and later resigned.

On August 20, 2008, Mark E. Smith posted this description of schools like State School in Columbus as being "horrific". In a February 1972 article in *Time* magazine he wrote this observation of one such school. "The rooms smelled of 'sweat, urine, excrement---and despair.' Residents in some cases were placed there with absolutely no reason to be there other than the fact they were misunderstood and misdiagnosed because of their disabilities."[5]

Families like the Reids, unable to care for children with emotional and physical challenges, often made them wards of the state. How many of these individuals had capable minds in good working order is unknown. How many of them resisted and overcame the traumatizing abuse Bill did and regained a full and useful life after State School is also unknown.

That children with non-critical medical disorders can still be placed in an institution in an enlightened nation such as America because they have cerebral palsy, muscular dystrophy, dwarfism or another medical handicap is shameful.

Another developmental center worker with an eleven year work experience described many of the staff as lazy and horribly abusive to residents. He spoke of hundreds of horror stories from the facility where he worked. His complaint was that negative reports were seldom or ever heard by the public while the negligent workers complaints about hard work were continually aired.

Where is our basic humanity? Where is our concern for families dealing with physically disabled children? For the hundreds of thousands of parents who do care for physically and emotionally disabled children, special recognition should be given and community support. Those unwilling or unable to cope with the challenges of care for the disabled must be addressed by the community.

Some changes have been made in the past forty-five years since Bill was sent to State School, but more are needed. Supposedly, the doors of State School closed years ago. However, clearly, they still haven't been entirely locked. The Columbus School has a new name with new guidelines for confinement.

An article in the Columbus Dispatch Friday, September 14, 2012, written by Allison Manning reported that a former worker at a facility run by Goodwill Columbus assaulted a 34-year-old Work and Behavioral Center client, knocking him to the floor. The staff member had to be pulled off the resident by another staff member at the facility. The client reportedly had bruises on his chest from the assault.

Because the staff member was a supervisor in charge of the client, the assault was listed as a felony. The Columbus police special-victims bureau states that delays in arrests are common in such cases. An investigation must first be conducted before a charge is filed. The client was a resident of the Columbus Developmental Center, the state-run residential facility located on W. Broad Street where Bill Reid spent his youth and early adult life. How much has really changed?

Conditions that Bill experienced in Ohio in the late 50's and early 60's were not by any means limited to Ohio. Currently, the State of California has an organized police unit specifically for the purpose of protecting severely handicapped individuals in custodial institutions. But, who will speak for them?

Hundreds of abuse cases have been reported since 2006 in California but only 2 arrests can be found on record by the unit since it began. One can only hope that increased public awareness and the testimonies of former clients in those places will bring about changes.

Tribute from Bill's Son

THERE are no better witnesses to the character of a person than those who live with them daily in a home. One of Bill's best witnesses is his son, Gary Reid. Gary paid tribute to his Dad's resilience and boldness when the author asked him for his opinion of his father. He wrote, "I am William Gary Reid and I am twenty-nine years old. My Dad has been the most influential person I have ever known apart from Jesus Christ. My dad has meant more to me than anyone. His life completely amazes me. I've heard about his life without Jesus Christ and I've seen his life with Christ. I'm glad I've never experienced any of the things my Dad went through during those early years."

"It amazes me seeing the life he lives and the difference God makes. I am happy to say I never went through anything my Dad went through. I grew up in Briggs Road Baptist Church. I had some difficulties growing up but my Dad was the first to say 'You know where you belong and where you need to be.' It was the smack in the back of the head I needed every once in a while to get me back on the right track. It's about knowing Jesus, the life before and the life afterward. I want to teach my children the same principles my Dad taught me and give them the same understanding he gave me."

"I think of my Dad when I sing this song: "Baptized, down with the Old Man, up with the New. Raised to walk in the way of Light and Truth. Didn't see no angels, just a few saints on the shore. But I felt like a newborn baby cradled up in the arms of the Lord. Amazing Grace."

Bill's Worldview

THE injured back Bill carried with him from childhood gradually grew worse. His injury at work complicated the condition. He finally agreed to go to a new doctor who sent him to a specialist. The surgeon told Bill that he could fix the problem in his back. After much prayer, Bill agreed to the operation knowing the danger of complete paralysis existed if the operation failed.

The operation was a success. Bill felt the presence of God in his healing while in the hospital. He was on cloud nine knowing God was in this. One night as he recovered in the hospital he awoke and had a vision of three angels in the room with him. Two were at the bottom of his feet and one was sitting in the window. When he awoke in the morning he accepted the experience as affirmation that God was with him.

"A fine Christian man told me when I told him about 3 angels that he had never seen any angels. I told him, I don't know but it happened to me. That's why I am telling you. I took different drugs in my past and people want to know why I am not in prison or they tell me I am crazy. They will tell me, 'How do you know this is God working?' Well, I'll tell you. It's how it works out. I went to see a man who had prayed to be saved. God already had him prepared when I got there. Lord, I don't know what to say to that person, but you do. If you want me to talk to them, you have to give me what I should say. Things come to my mind and mouth that I would never have thought about. "

Two days passed and all the equipment had been removed from him. He was told he could go home the next morning. That night something happened. His blood pressure suddenly dropped. He began to hallucinate. A nurse came in, saw his condition, and ran for a machine to remove excess fluid from his body. Bill was weak from the ordeal.

The doctor attended him the next morning and announced that he could not go home. He would have to go to a nursing home to recuperate. Once more it seemed to him that God had something different for him to do. A nursing home was found and Bill was transferred to it in great pain. He was placed in a private room. True to his habit of discovering what God was doing in his life, Bill began to pray for people to come into his room.

"Once when I was on my own I went to a church and they dragged me down the aisle and prayed over me. Nothing happened. They told me I was full of the devil and God didn't love me. These people were downright hateful. If you didn't believe the way they were you were going to hell. I was cautious not to get around this sort of people. I didn't like to interfere with people so I stayed away from them."

"I learned to let people believe the way they want to believe. There were self-redeemed preachers. They never went to school but picked up a Bible and let it say what it wants. Harold Smith taught me the word of God. He taught me that if you can't trust anybody, you can trust God. It may not be any way you want but it will be the right way. God gives you the ability to say things about Him, you say them. He will show you how to say them. You give Him the glory and praise for what He's done in your life. It may not turn out the way you want but if it is God's way, it will be alright."

"God has given me opportunity to talk to doctors and nurses. When our grandchild was born prematurely, doctors told us that he was going to die. I told them, 'Only if God wants the baby to die. If God wants this baby to live, it will live.' Our grandchild is healthy and growing and the doctors and nurses respect me for my belief. God has a purpose and a reason. When another day would pass and the baby lived I would tell them, 'Today's another day and the baby is still alive and improving. The baby is going to make it.' I would pray, 'Lord, you have to help him.' The baby lived. We prayed and others prayed with me and the baby lived. People will tell me, 'I'm praying for your baby. The Lord will take care of him. God knows what will happen. Give God the glory and the praise.'"

"God would put the right people in the right areas to do what He wanted. I learned what knife to use and what piece went where. I learned not to waste any part of the meat. If I didn't know how to do it, I would butter up to somebody and say, 'You do such a good job. Show me how to do it.' They would show me. I learned how to put old potatoes into water and dissolve them and put them with new potatoes and make them look nice when they came out. People would buy them."

"I had to learn to see how God works. Sometimes I get so excited people think I am crazy. I tell them you aren't listening to God. When I lie down at night and pray and I listen for God's small quiet voice, He speaks to me. He shows me at times. He does things in my life at times. I know God created everything. I ask him to heal me. But, God says to me, 'I'm using you the way you are. I can heal you but I use you the way you are.'"

"It amazed me what God put in my mouth to say. I could have gone to hell many times from cars or bullets and no one cared for me. I thank God for keeping me from going there. I tried to go there twice and God spoke to me in those times."

"It amazed me what God did and how he did it. I got through that school because God was in it. I didn't care about living or dying but God did. He had a plan for me and State School was in it. God arranged circumstances to show me,

"This is where I want you to go. This is what I want you to do." God was working on me even though I didn't know who He was nor did I believe in Him. He still took care of me. I should have been dead for all the trouble I got into and the alcohol and drugs I used. Instead, God brought me through everything. I am so very grateful I didn't' die and got through it. I am so grateful. God kept telling me after I met Him, 'I forgive you. I love you. I have great plans for you'."

"Westside Church where I began to worship only had seven people when Harold Smith came there as its pastor but he touched thousands of people through that church over the span of his ministry there. There were doctors, lawyers, important people, even a ping pong tournament winner who were changed in that church. Harold Smith took me under his wing and taught me to love people the way God loved me."

"It amazed me how God would say, 'Bill doesn't believe in me or love me but someday I'm going to touch his life and he will love me.' From that I learned never to take people for granted regardless of their past or present circumstances. I learned to do my part and leave the rest to God. God will do His part. As my kids were born and later my six grandchildren, I would say to each of them, 'I wonder what you will be like 20 years from now. God loves you. Jesus loves you. The Holy Spirit loves you and I love you, too.' When my children were born I would lie down and talk to each of my kids at night and tell them that God loved them."

"I would tell people I met that God doesn't guarantee a tomorrow. You better be ready to meet Him today. Tomorrow may never come for you. You can do nothing yourself, but God can do anything through you. If you don't believe it, let me tell you what he did for me."

"A Doctor said to me, 'Something tells me you don't need to be here.' I told him, 'It wasn't me. It was the presence of God. The Lord has me here for a reason.' I began to share Christ with the doctors and nurses. Opportunity after opportunity came in the nursing home. It was amazing. People would sit on my bed and listen to me. The lady who cleaned my room came in and I told her about Christ and how much he cared for her. I went to therapy and shared Christ with everyone down there. I got to pray with doctors and share with them. People were saved and changed. I learned that when you want to be used by God, He will use you. I really try to convince other Christians of that everywhere I go."

"The Bible has been my guide since my life changed. "The Bible says, 'Behold I stand at the door and knock.' Revelation 3:20 If I listen and not say a word God will speak through a preacher, a radio. There is a word for me. It may be one word or many. It speaks to my heart. His word does not return unto him void."

"The Bible says, 'God so loved the world...' John 3:16 God loves everyone no matter who they are or what they have done. Here is God speaking to me. No matter how bad I have been in life, God loves me. It makes me realize God's grace and mercy. I tell people, 'God loves you. He will forgive all sin.' I did some awful things. God would say to me, 'I don't care about what you did but what you do right now. Give me your life and let me show you what I will do. I'm helping you and you don't even know it. Listen, I was there when you were at that point.' Recognize God's presence and how he works. It's amazing how the Lord works through people like us. We don't deserve it but He works through us."

"I've heard these words over and over, 'The Lord is my shepherd...' Psalm 23:1 When I listen to them I understand that I shall want no other shepherd. He is the most important person in my life. I listen to the Bible on tape and ask God to show me something different that I did not know and He will show me. I will call up my pastor and tell him, 'The Lord showed me this.' Lord, who can use this scripture beside me. God will bring a name to mind. I call them and tell them and they say to me, 'Billy, you don't have any idea what that meant to me. I needed that today.' I do this a lot."

"Let God open the door. Don't open it yourself. If you open the door you will get into a lot of trouble. When someone says to me, 'I've had a rotten day today. I feel like dying.' I ask them, 'If you did die where would you go?'

Give the Lord the praise. You have to give him the glory and praise or God won't honor what you do. He paid an awesome price on the cross. He is a jealous God and when we step outside of His will we got a whole bunch of trouble. God will blow doors off for you because He loves you."

Postlude

Born for trouble, filled with anger and bitterness, physically and mentally challenged, physically and sexually abused, driven to suicide, Bill Reid's life was transformed in a single moment. His troubles ended, his rage drained, his nightmares of abuse ended, his mind was challenged and hope restored. Others have survived crushing circumstances. Some have left their mark in relative obscurity; others have gained the spotlight of fame through their service. Few have overcome the challenges Bill Reid did and consistently remained in such high esteem by those around them. There's a paradox in the promises of Christ that not all who follow him will be protected from hardship and suffering. God uses tragedies like those Bill experienced to extend our ministry to a skeptical world and show that He is able to make "lemonade out of lemons." It is true that "...the God of all comfort; who comforts us in all our tribulation, that we may be able to comfort them which are in any trouble, by the comfort wherewith we ourselves are comforted of God." 2 Corinthians

1:4 Sometimes, God's blessings come through our suffering and not our accomplishments.

In spite of their shared difficulties, Bill and Sheena Reid continue to live a servant life helping others in Christ's power. They have found meaning and purpose sharing God's love in God's love.

Bill summed up his worldview this way: "I prefer not to talk about the bad things that happened to me but if the things done to me will help someone find peace with God, I will. Maybe they will see the things God did for me and it will help them to find a full and meaningful life too."

"I was at State School for seven years. I'm not sure about all the things that happened so long ago. I have forgotten a lot of it. I was thirteen years old when I went there. I'm not proud of who I was or what I did. I'm here to tell you what God did in my life and how he changed me. I believe in miracles because I am a miracle. Before I was born the doctor told my mother that I was dead. We're going to take the baby. We're sorry it happened. They gave my mother pills and three hours later I was born."

"The frustration I had from not understanding my disabilities and the anger I had because others did not understand my needs filled me with rage. When children called me names, I fought back. By age eight I was uncontrollable. I couldn't learn. If only someone had understood my needs and introduced me to know Christ when I was eight years old, I never would have gone through what I did. I want to tell everyone about Christ when they're young. Their hearts are impressionable and they're willing to listen and turn to God."

"I've been blessed since I've been saved. I have a wife, Sheena Reid, a son, William Reid, and a daughter, Rebecca Reid. William is twenty-nine years old. He has three children. I am a grandfather. My son served his country for one term in the military. He now teaches a bible study and sings in church. His wife is very sweet and she's grown as a Christian."

"When we go to my son's house at Christmas I sit down with the grandkids and read the bible and pray and sing Happy birthday to Jesus and the kids open their gifts and we eat and talk about old times and good times and what we would change for our Christmas. We are a close family. We love each other. We have few problems aside from financial ones. My son lives in Columbus and works as a bookkeeper. He supervises over thirty people. His wife works for an electrician."

"Our daughter, Rebecca, was married and has been divorced. We have opened our home to her and her baby. We continue to give her the support and guidance she needs to find the direction God wants for her in life."

"Sheena and I have been married thirty years. Much has happened to us but the Lord helped us through each trial. Very early in my new life in Christ a Christian woman told me about a promise God made. "Fear not, for I *am* with you;

Be not dismayed, for I *am* your God. I will strengthen you, Yes, I will help you, I will uphold you with My righteous right hand." (Isaiah 41:10) She told me that I should let the Bible speak to me for it is a living Word from God. I learned that God is saying that no matter what I am going through He will go through it with me.

"Now, whenever I feel threatened or someone makes an unkind remark to me, I say to the Lord, 'Lord, you said it so now I want you to show me. I'm not asking to be set free from my danger but I'm asking you to strengthen me and tell me what to do." When a man held a knife to my throat, and threatened to beat me up for talking about God, He intervened and helped me and showed me what to do. It seemed that I could hear God saying, 'See, you can trust me'!"

"When I ran across someone with a problem, I would tell them about this promise and tell them to let the Bible speak to them. I repeated that promise to thousands of people. A few lines below that promise God made another promise that I've turned to time after time. For I, the LORD your God, will hold your right hand, Saying to you, 'Fear not, I will help you.' Isaiah 41:13 That says to me that God's hand will save me and keep me. Through it all I've learned to trust him.

I have a family that loves me. I had a job for seventeen years that provided for my needs. I have a house. I have a retirement. God is the One who gave me everything. He has always blessed and strengthened me.

"I haven't spoken as much as I used to. I helped my wife care for my mother who was an Alzheimer patient. I spoke in prisons, churches, and the open streets, wherever I could find a place to talk about God's grace. I haven't spent as much time meeting people on the streets of Columbus as I used to spend. I can't count the number of people I met and shared the hope and joy of Jesus with on those streets. I thank God he gave me the opportunity to find Christ and change my life.

"I've seen God work in my life. Miracle after miracle He's done in my presence. People say God will heal you if you trust in Him. God uses me the way I am. I still talk to people about God. I try to convince them to turn to Christ. People have a lot of respect for me. I stand up for what I believe. I just tell them how God changed my life. God is bigger than all our needs.

"The words of this song describe how I feel. "Who Am I that you would love me so gently? Who am I that you would recognize my name. Amazing Grace. Grace, Grace, God's Grace". I want people through my story to know Jesus. I want it to bring Him glory. I want my story to honor God. I want it to point people to Christ and give Him the glory."[1]

---

1. www.Ohio History Central. Asylum for the Education of Idiotic and Imbecile Youth
2. www.columbuslibrary.org
3. www.ahrcnyc.org/aboutus/files/History_Of_AHRC.pdf p.12
4. http://blogsnap.wordpress.com/2008/12/05geraldo-rivera
5. 5Echoes of Willowbrook. Posted on August 20, 2008 by Mark E. Smith